YOUR HEART'S DESIRES

A LOOK AT LOVE, SEX, GRACE, FORGIVENESS, AND ACCEPTANCE

CHRISTINA LEEMAN, MPH

Your Heart's Desires
by Christina Leeman
Copyright © 2025 Christina Leeman

All rights reserved. This book is protected under the copyright laws of the United States of America. This book may not be copied or reprinted for commercial gain or profit.

Unless otherwise identified, Scripture taken from the Holy Bible, *New Living Translation*, copyright © 1996, 2004, 2015 by Tyndale House Foundation. Used by permission of Tyndale House Publishers, Inc., Carol Stream, Illinois 60188. All rights reserved.

Scripture quotations marked ESV are taken from *The ESV® Bible* (The Holy Bible, English Standard Version®). Copyright © 2001 by Crossway, a publishing ministry of Good News Publishers. All rights reserved.

Scripture quotations marked MSG are taken from *THE MESSAGE*, copyright © 1993, 2002, 2018 by Eugene H. Peterson. Used by permission of NavPress. All rights reserved. Represented by Tyndale House Publishers, Inc. All rights reserved.

Scripture quotations marked NASB are taken from the *New American Standard Bible®*, Copyright © 1960, 1971, 1977, 1995, 2020 by The Lockman Foundation. All rights reserved.

Scripture quotations marked NIV are taken from the *HOLY BIBLE, NEW INTERNATIONAL VERSION®*. Copyright © 1973, 1978, 1984

Scripture quotations marked ERV are taken from the *Easy-to-Read-Bible* by International Bible Society. Used by permission of Zondervan Publishing House. All rights reserved. Copyright © 2006 by Bible League international

Scripture quotations marked CEV are taken from the *Contemporary English Version®* Copyright © 1995 American Bible Society. All rights reserved.

ISBN 978-1-63360-310-3

For Worldwide Distribution   Printed in the U.S.A.

Urban Press
P.O. Box 8881
Pittsburgh, PA 15221-0881 USA
412.646.2780
www.urbanpress.us

Table of Contents

Introduction	v
Chapter 1: Healthy Relationship First	1
Chapter 2: That Thing Called Love ... What It Is Not	18
Chapter 3: That Thing Called Love ... What Love Is	27
Chapter 4: The Ultimate True Love	38
Chapter 5: Sex Uncovered	45
Chapter 6: Your Period ... The Menstrual Cycle Explained	54
Chapter 7: Your Brain On Sex	59
Chapter 8: Eight Reasons Why You May Get It on Before Marriage	70
Chapter 9: Sex Out of Order	85
Chapter 10: The Aftershock of Sex	99
Chapter 11: God's Design for Sex	110
Chapter 12: The Truth about God's Grace and Forgiveness	116
Chapter 13: More than Breasts and Booty ... A Woman's Worth	130
Chapter 14: No More Fear of Missing Out	136
Chapter 15: Abstinence	142
Chapter 16: Lead Us Not Into Temptation	156
Chapter 17: Help Is Available	162
Refences	167

To protect the privacy of those involved, names, locations, and certain identifying details have been changed.

Introduction

Sex is *everywhere*. It is almost impossible to watch television, go to the movies, or listen to music without seeing or hearing a message with sexual undertones. The world says sex is good because it feels good, it strengthens relationships, and alleviates stress—and again, it feels so good. So why would our parents and leaders in church tell us to "Wait until you're married to have sex"? If you were told to wait until marriage to have sex, were you ever given the reason?

Some may have encouraged you to wait, saying that it is a sin, or because you may experience an unplanned pregnancy. While these are valid reasons why God wants you to wait until marriage, there is much more to it and truly, God wants the best for you. I wrote this book to share the biblical and surprisingly biological reasons why saving sex for marriage is the best decision.

I will never forget the sadness and tears of women I have met, helped, and prayed over the six years of working at a pregnancy resource center. I met women who were hurting, love-starved, and broken. Many of them had not yet embraced the truth about their worth and value, were not aware of God's acceptance and immense love for them, and didn't know the truth about sex. I expressed my love and care for every single one of them and extended grace to them along with God's truth to help them in their situations. I was not there to condemn the women or berate their choices. I was there to help them the best way I could and give them the facts so they could make the right choices. I gave them the gift of knowledge, especially about God's love for them and Jesus' sacrifice on their behalf.

What's more, I shared with them God's design for sex (the biblical and biological reasons and why He wants us to wait for marriage). We delve into what love is according to the love chapter,1 Corinthians 13 and the truth of God's love for us (the ultimate true love that is Jesus). Those women were the catalyst for this book because I know there are many more out there who have no one to turn to. This book will educate, embolden, and enlighten women concerning healthy relationships, God's grace, forgiveness, and acceptance.

I wrote this book because I didn't always make the best decisions before marriage and I want to help other women (and men) make the right choices, to know and be in God's will, and to be spared unnecessary pain and consequences. I want to help God's creations to experience life the way He has designed and He purposed it to be. Ladies, we are more than breasts and booty (more on that later)! We are beautifully and wonderfully made in His image. His purpose for us is not to use sex as a means of selfish fulfillment or to turn ourselves (or allow ourselves to be turned) into sex objects; He does not intend us to derive our value from sex.

God loves us and wants what is best for us! We are to live an abundant life in Him, and this book is a guide toward an abundant life by giving the truth in love about healthy relationships, love, and God's design for sex.

Speaking of love, I would love to hear from you as you are reading this book! I invite you to share your thoughts and experiences, and to let me know how this book has impacted you. You can share it on social media with the hashtag #LoveSexGraceForgiveness or for more privacy email me at Christina@shewhohonors.com. I look forward to hearing from you. Know that I am praying for you as you journey toward truth.

Dear Lord,

Thank you for all that you are! Thank You for the gift of grace that is in Your Son, Jesus. Thank You for this precious woman who is reading this book. I pray that she has an open mind and heart to absorb the truth about healthy relationships, love, and Your design for sex. I pray she realizes that she is worth the wait and embraces Your love for her. I pray she knows that the information in this book is to help and not harm her. Help her have the courage to obey your Word. In Jesus' name I pray, amen.

>Love ya!
>Christina Leeman
>July 2025
>Pittsburgh, PA

Chapter 1

Healthy Relationship First

*"Oh, let me warn you, sisters in Jerusalem,
by the gazelles, yes, by all the wild deer: Don't
excite love, don't stir it up, until the time is
ripe—and you're ready."*
(Song of Songs 2:7 MSG).

Romance is found in the Bible. The Song of Songs is ancient poetry filled with beautiful descriptions of love, desire, and sex. The stanzas ebb and flow with longing and passionate wordplay between a woman and man, taking the reader from courtship to marriage and finally the intimate sexual bonding between husband and wife.

God knows our longing and heart's desires to be accepted, loved, and to love. The Song of Songs is proof of His knowledge of our desire and need for romance. Sexual desires and sexuality are part of our makeup, a melodious sensual pleasure experience when the time is ripe—and we are ready.

No quiz, apps, dating site, or calendars can tell the exact time love is ready. But there is a process that may help start developing healthy relationships.

Healthy Relationships

God created us to be in healthy relationships with others. Relationships are important for spiritual, personal and mental growth. A good relationship gives life. Positive and affirming relationships add value to our lives. A good relationship promotes positive emotions and well-being. Unhealthy connections drain our spirits, resulting in a toxic bond which contradicts God's design of relationship.

Romantic relationships take time to blossom. TV, movies, and books depict quick hook-ups, two people in love in just a week's time. All those are false portrayals! Those made-up stories stimulate our feel-good hormone receptors, Dopamine (we will talk about dopamine later), influencing our brains to keep watching. Be alert, for what we watch or read impacts our thinking.

Pay attention "perfect man or perfect woman list makers." You know who you are. You have a list, perhaps only mental, of what your perfect mate will be and even look like. My advice to you is simple: Throw your list away! There is no such thing as a perfect person for you, except God. And you are certainly not the answer to someone else's perfect list, for you know who and how you are. A list-maker person is destined to have their quest end in loneliness in their later years. The list maker then may settle for whomever they can find or be a serial relationshiper (yes, I made that word up).

By the way, let me share with you that I am in an interracial relationship. My husband is a white man, and I am a black woman. After he asked me out at least five times, I finally went on a date with him, the best date ever. We have been married for 23 years. It's not a perfect marriage, but God chose us for each other. Race does not matter in a relationship. Ethan and I have similar likes and dislikes and not so similar likes and dislikes, just like same race couples!

There are good and bad in every race, for foolishness is no respecter of persons. I say that because he would not have been on my list if I had composed one. You don't want to be with the person you concoct in your mind. You want the person God has for you, for God knows what you need and who your spouse needs. Your list should have only one thing on it and that is: "the person God has for me."

Before we delve into the love-and-sex parts of the book, I want to talk about being in relationships first. Healthy relationships may go through various levels. Each level brings up important questions to be answered before moving further on in the relationship.

Relationship Level 1: Attraction

Laboratory work slows down during the Christmas season. A group of us specimen processors laugh and chat. We are in a good mood, because it's a light night for specimens. Suddenly something drops beside me. Then something hits me on the top of my head. I see it is a plastic cap we use to close test tubes. My coworker sees the flying caps too.

I look around, then I look straight ahead. On the other side of the room nestled together in their own little group were Ethan and a few other male co-workers. Ethan, with a sly grin on his cute face, looks straight at me.

My coworker and I stand up and yell, "Stop it!"

"I know it was you who threw that," I yell across the lab to Ethan.

"What are you talking about?" he hollers back, trying to look cool.

Standing there with hands on my hips, I give him the look only a woman can give.

"You keep throwing specimen caps over here and one hit me on the head."

"That wasn't me," he cooly states. His friends sit there with knowing smiles on their faces.

"Quit it," I said confidently. I sit back down. My co-worker sits down, laughing. We continue talking about various things, laughing and enjoying each other's company (this was before smartphones were invented). But I keep on glancing over where Ethan sits. I see he is looking at me! Ethan is handsome and intelligent because apparently throwing (clean) specimen caps at a young lady works! We have been married for 23 years as I write.

That event wasn't the only one that attracted me to Ethan. His persistence, confidence, intelligence, looks, and manner attracted me to him. After we started working in the same part of the lab, Ethan asked me out for the first time.

I said no.

Ethan: "Want to go out with us for breakfast?" (our work schedule was 8 p.m. to 4 a.m.)

Me: "No."

"Want to go out with us for wings?"

"No."

Ethan three months later: "I want to make you dinner."

Me: "Yes."

I'll never forget the day of our first date. That afternoon, I went to the store to get some things for the date and realized my watch had stopped! I didn't have Ethan's phone number to let him know I would be late. The year was 1999, and smart phones weren't available then so I couldn't text him. Then again, he hadn't given me his phone number!

I raced home, got showered, put on a cute black skirt and purple top (yes, I remember the outfit), did my hair, put a little eye makeup on, and ran out the door. I drove over the speed limit to get to his apartment. Fortunately, he lived close to me, but still I arrived at his apartment two-and-a-half hours late! I explained why I was late. I felt badly for the poor guy thought I stood him up. Although it was a rough start, it was the best date ever. I'm happy I said yes to Ethan.

Attraction is an interesting phenomenon. What is attractive to one person may be different to another. Attraction can be something small like their laugh, to something much larger like their love for God. Whatever it is, there is something about that person that draws you towards them, sometimes for reasons unknown.

I like the definition of attract from the *Oxford American Dictionary*: 1) to draw towards itself by an unseen force; 2) to get the attention of; or 3) to arouse the interest or pleasure of. *To draw towards itself by an unseen force.* The unseen force reminds me of how God operates. I know God chose Ethan for me. The various trials we've experienced in our marriage are evidence of that truth, for without him, I'm not sure I could have made it through. And the same can be said for him.

Sometimes we don't know what may attract us to others, the unseen force stimulating the attraction. While attraction is real, sometimes the attraction doesn't mean the other person is the "one" for us. For example, an attraction may be pheromone related. Pheromones are substances which are secreted externally by an individual and received by a second individual of the same species.[1] Scientific studies show a man's pheromones can affect a woman's mood and mate selection. It's not wise to rely solely or primarily on this pheromone attraction. A pheromone, like other chemicals our bodies produce, has a job to do, but it has no values. A pheromone can't tell if the person we're attracted to is right or wrong for us.

We still need to learn more about this person and that requires using our mind, not just relying on our heart or feeling. This includes using discernment, observing their behaviors, learning more about them before getting involved with them too deeply. A relationship doesn't start at this attraction phase. Attraction's job is to make us aware of the other person.

Relationship Level 2: Casual and Observing

The casual-and-observing level is when we are learning more about our potential boyfriend/girlfriend/friend. Observe and pay attention to them and how they act in various surroundings and situations.

If working with the person, note their work ethic. Watch how they treat their co-workers. Eat lunch with them in group settings.

If you are in the same class in college or school, study them. Pay attention to their character and personality. Information is gathered and questions are answered by asking and observing their behavior. Here are some questions to consider at this second level:

- Are they funny, kind, calm?
- Are they usually happy and in a good mood?
- Are they always in a bad mood or moody?
- How is their work ethic?
- Are they compassionate?
- Do they complain a lot?
- Are they regularly late?
- Are they self-centered?
- Are they sarcastic?
- Do they like school?
- Is school important to them?

These questions will be answered over time. Observe in order to identify their actions, weaknesses, and strong points before getting closer. If their character is disquieting or concerning, stay in the casual/observing level for a while longer. Don't risk your future and heart by getting closer. Protect your heart. Be careful and if possible, try not to be alone with them when you are at this level.

Relationship Level 3: Getting Closer

After you observe their characteristics and personality with no obvious concerns or questionable issues—and hopefully they have been observing you—the relationship can move to the getting-closer level. In this level, you start to spend more one-on-one time with them. Trust grows. You learn more about their values and feelings.

Questions are important. When we are questioning something, we seek answers, which give us knowledge. Using answers combined with our feelings and logic to make a sound decision is wise. Wisdom from God helps us to thrive in life.

> Give instruction to a wise man, and he will be still wiser; teach a righteous man, and he will increase in learning. The fear of the Lord is the beginning of wisdom, and the knowledge of the Holy One is insight. For by me your days will be multiplied, and years will be added to your life. If you are wise, you are wise for yourself; if you scoff, you alone will bear it (Proverbs 9:9-12, ESV).

Some good questions at this stage are:

- What are their passions?
- What do they value?
- Do they know and believe in Jesus as their Lord and Savior?
- If so, do they bear fruits of the Spirit? (patience, kindness, gentleness, self-control, etc.)

- Are they jealous of your friends? (red flag)
- What are their priorities?
- Do they get angry easily? (red flag)
- What are their goals/dreams?
- How is their relationship with their family?
- Do they have many exes?
- Are they controlling? (red flag)
- Are you starting to see negative patterns? (red flag)

If their values and feelings don't align with yours, if they are negative and hurtful to you or others, stop the relationship *now*. If the answer is yes to the red flag questions above, stop the relationship *now*. These characteristics are usually signs of abusive people. It is hard to change someone, so please don't try to make it a mission to change their character. They may need professional help, not the kind of help you can give them.

At this level, it is not wise to introduce sex into the relationship, especially if there are red flags. Sex is defined as any act that causes arousal, not just intercourse. Having sex involves hormones that cause bonding and makes it even harder to leave that person if you need to do so. Sex lulls us—especially women—into a false sense of trust. The best time for sex is when you are married.

When you engage in sexual activity at any relationship level, something is lost. Sex often becomes the focal point and even though the relationship may not be a right fit, sex can deceive you into thinking it is—at least for a little while. There are a few chapters later in the book that will deal exclusively with sex.

As Christ followers, we are to be wary of getting close to someone of a different faith or an unbeliever. When I say different faith, I'm not talking about denomination. I'm referring to different beliefs in other gods or religious systems. Those other beliefs are from the devil and are demonic. That sounds harsh, but if the religion is not from God, then who is it from? And their goal is not to respect your Christian faith, it is usually to take you away from it.

> Don't team up with those who are unbelievers. How can righteousness be a partner with wickedness? How can light live with darkness? What harmony can there be between Christ and the devil? How can a believer be a partner with an unbeliever? And what union can there be between God's temple and idols? For we are the temple of the living God. As God said: 'I will live in them and walk among them. I will be their God, and they will be my people. Therefore, come out from among unbelievers, and separate yourselves from them, says the Lord. Don't touch their filthy things, and I will welcome you. And I will be your Father, and you will be my sons and daughters" (2 Corinthians 6:14-18).

God says this for a reason. He loves you and

wants the best for you. When you obey and do what he says, life is successful and prosperous, and you thrive. When you disobey and do not do what He says, it causes destruction in your life—and that goes for all of us who are His children by faith in Christ.

If you end up in a relationship with an unbeliever, it won't be an easy relationship because God will not be a part of it. A cord with three strings is not easily broken and that means if you want your marriage relationship to work, you need it to involve you, your partner, and God as an active participant and helper. Please don't pursue a relationship based on how he makes you "feel" because those feelings don't last. Save yourself the drama and heartbreak and don't continue the relationship.

Level 4: Trusting

You casually observe them, like what you see, and start getting closer. In the closer level, you find out more about them and hopefully like the answers to their questions. Their values and beliefs align with yours.

In this third level, trust is earned by being genuine. You see the real person and accept them. I still caution against sex, which includes intimate touching, long hugs, back rubs, etc. These physical actions cause certain hormones to do their job and bring a false sense of trust and security. You want to trust the other party based on actual circumstances and experience, not on a bodily response. Again, I'll go into more detail in the sex chapter.

Some appropriate questions during this stage are:

- Are their feelings clear to you?

- Do they allow you to be real and honest?
- Can you talk to them about their strengths and weaknesses, and they don't get upset? Do you?
- Will they accept help? Will you?
- Are they willing to grow? Are you?
- Are they judgmental and critical of you or others? Are you?
- Do they pray?
- Do they read the Bible?

Obviously, these questions help assess you too. You expect others not to act a certain way, but do you act that way? When we are in relationships, we want to bring out our best selves. A relationship won't be healthy if you carry unresolved baggage, hurt, pain, or stereotypes into it. If you have unresolved issues or problems, seek help from God and others. Pray, read the Bible looking for answers, seek professional advice, or talk to a good friend. Get those root issues resolved before getting into or seeking a serious relationship; it will make life easier and better.

Sometimes people are in relationships but are stuck at certain levels. Or they get into serial relationships and always break up at a certain point. When this happens, there are unresolved issues, a root cause which needs to be worked on before they attempt to maintain a serious relationship.

Root Causes

Collins English Dictionary defines root cause as *the fundamental reason for the occurrence of a problem.*

According to the *Merriam-Webster Dictionary,* fundamental is defined as *serving as an original or generating source.* Some examples of root causes are trauma, a difficult childhood, feeling unloved, absent parents, abuse, sexual trauma, generational problems that aren't stopped, boundaries not taught (like saying no), permissive parents, authoritative parents, racism, sexism, etc. Root causes are unhealed wounds obtained through hurtful actions, words, or situations that were detrimental to your development.

If you or someone you know has experienced some of these things and hasn't received any help, I suggest you get help for them immediately. I am so sorry for what you or they have been through and will be praying for you all if you have experienced these things.

Acknowledge the wounds. Ask Jesus to show them to you if you are unsure what unhealed hurts you have deep down. Please understand that God is the ultimate healer. I recommend the book *Soul Care* by Dr. Rob Reimer to help heal the wounds in your soul. *Soul Care* changed my life. I don't want to bring up these things so you can dwell on the past and remain stuck in the victim role. I repeat: Get the help you need to move forward and live the life God intended!

Finding out the root cause of an issue is critical. Even businesses do root cause analysis for erratic behaviors that are outside of their normal parameters, Events like misdiagnosis and known issues without resolutions are just two examples. Here are steps to help find out the root cause of some issues and or behaviors that are manifesting, a root cause analysis.[2]

1. **Brainstorm**. Grab a pen and paper and jot down the issues and behaviors that have led to the same negative outcomes. This will help to define the problem or problems. Pray for the Lord to help reveal these issues.
2. **Analyze.** How long has this behavior been in action or have you been having these issues? Bring family and friends in on this to get their input. How has this been impacting your life?
3. **Get specific.** Give a name to the cause factor, thing, place and/or person that leads to these issues or behaviors. There is usually more than one.
4. **Identify the root cause.** Why does the causal factor, thing, place, or person exist? What is the real reason for these issues or behaviors? Most human problems come from basic needs like security, identity, purpose, self-worth, belonging, and being loved.
5. **Resolve/solve the problem.** Talk to a trusted pastor, counselor, or spiritual mentor. Talk to a Christian counselor/psychologist. Pray for Jesus to reveal solutions to you.

One of the best solutions available is getting

to know God and Jesus. God has permitted these needs to help us realize that He is the only one who will always be there for us. Jesus is perfect, we humans are not. We are broken and eventually someone will fail us, but God will never fail us.

Acknowledge the wounds. Ask Jesus to show them to you if you are unsure what unhealed hurts you have deep down. As I said earlier, accept the important truth that God is the ultimate healer.

We all know of someone who has some issues. If that someone is a friend, be a good friend and confront then on this issue in a loving way. Don't be offended if they lash out, for sometimes the truth stings and people can't handle it. God knows your heart. Speak the truth in love to help and encourage your friend in need.

If you are reading this and think, *Wow this is me,* then I pray you seek God's guidance and wisdom, and get the help you need to uncover the issue.

The trusting level is when the relationship is getting serious with thoughts of spending your lives together. However, I still warn you not to have any sexual relations. Yes, a serious, lasting relationship can happen without having sex. There are many emotional and physical consequences of sex out of order. Some are serious, some fatal, and others life changing. I repeat this often for a reason. I'm serious about this sex thing, and God is too.

Level 5: Developed

The developed level is reached by knowing each other well, accepting each other's quirks, and moving on into a mature relationship in which both of you are growing in positive ways in the relationship. At this level, you are understanding each other and one another's needs. You are in love and may even know the other's love language (another good book to read: *The 5 Love Languages* by Gary Chapman). Trust is earned and you both are willing to work through conflicts in a healthy and mature way.

Conflicts are a natural part of any relationship and occur because each person has a different goal. When you experience conflict, actively listen to each other's goal. Repeat what is said to show understanding. Realize why you have differing goals. Recognize each other's pain, which are disguised as defense mechanisms—arguing, escaping, etc. If you can't speak because the pain is too strong, give each other some space. Pray for the Holy Spirit to invade your heart with peace. When the pain of the conflict dies down, talk it out. Be respectful of the fact that your goals are different. Pray for Jesus to give you the wisdom to navigate the conflict so you can figure out together how to make each goal happen.

A healthy, loving relationship takes time, mindfulness, prayer, God, good communication, and energy from both people. It isn't a healthy, loving relationship if only one person is doing all the work. Make God the foundation of your relationship. He provides strength. When God is involved, your lives will thrive and prosper.

Think on These Things

- You can ask yourself the questions during each stage. Do a self-evaluation. Write down your answers in a journal.
- If you have been in serial relationships, take some time to seek what may be an issue in your life. There is a root cause for everything.
- Physical intimacy and sex will hinder positive relationship growth. Save sex and physical intimacy for marriage.
- Relationships take time and effort from both parties.
- Strive for positive, healthy relationships for both friendships and boyfriend/girlfriend relationships.
- Know your value and worth and don't settle for less.
- God as the foundation in any relationship makes it stronger.

Chapter 2

The Thing Called Love . . . What It's Not

"How beautiful is your love, my sister, my bride! How much better is your love than wine, and the fragrance of your oils than all kinds of spices!"
(Song of Songs 4:10, NASB).

Love is a primary want and need. Psychological theories have been created to examine and explain this strong desire and one of these approaches is called Maslow's Hierarchy of Needs. This theory consists of a pyramid with eight levels. Maslow's Hierarchy of Needs explains that we are motivated by protection, food, love, self-awareness, etc. at different levels in our development. A sense of belonging and love needs are one level. If we don't fulfill those needs, it's hard to move to the next level. This philosophy is not new, for love is the theme throughout the Bible. It all starts with love.

Newborn babies need to be held and loved

or they will fail to thrive. Children engage in behaviors to garner attention and love from their parents or caregivers. Teens and young adults make wild choices for love, or what they think is love. Adults do crazy things for love too. Love, how it feels and what it does, is the primary motivator for many of our actions.

Pay attention to the statement I just wrote: "what they think is love." Love is more than a feeling. Love is an action word. Love gives.

Be aware of lust, what it is and does. Lust is not love. Lust is selfish, short-lived, hormone-driven, mostly sexual, and almost addictive. Lust gets. Lust, a toxic emotion, drains life out of people. It isn't healthy. Please exit the relationship if you are in a lust relationship. It will hurt for some time after, but with the right people, help, and distance, life will get back to normal.

What Is Love?

As I stated above, many have studied and attempted to describe love. What is the meaning of love? How do we know we are in love? Does he or she love me? Does love do this? Is this love? We have all had a question or two about love some time in our lives. How do we find out the answers or know the truth?

There are many definitions of love. According to the *Oxford American Dictionary*, love (noun) has seven different meanings. Included in that definition is love, a verb, which has a few meanings too. The best definitions, answers, and guides for love are found in the Bible. The Bible itself is love. God loves us so much He had the Bible written to help us navigate life. The Bible gives us instructions to follow to get the best life possible!

Love is a feeling, an emotion, but it is also an action word. Love makes you do things, sometimes crazy things. Many characteristics make up what love is, but there are characteristics that love will never be.

1. Love is not jealous.

Jealousy is a toxic emotion that causes stress and childish emotions. Children get jealous easily because their brains aren't fully developed and their world centers around them. Children are egocentric. As an adult, you learn the world doesn't revolve around you. (At least, I hope you learned that). To be blunt: jealousy is a negative and selfish emotion.

Jealousy is not healthy and will zap the life out of a relationship. Death to a relationship and spiritual death to the person is the end game of jealousy. It counters what God does when He brings life to a relationship. Jealousy is defined in the *Oxford American Dictionary* as *feeling or showing resentment toward a person whom one thinks as a rival*. Admit it, you may sometimes think it's flattering when in your new relationship the other party is jealous of other men or women looking at you or flirting with you. But when we stop and think about it, it shows a bit of insecurity, and it is not a healthy way of thinking or acting for either party in a relationship.

Love is not jealous or envious of anyone. In a loving, healthy, developed relationship, there are no rivals.

2. Love is not boastful or proud.

"My man always gets me the finest things. My girlfriend has an awesome body." Those statements are examples of what is called boasting. Boasting is speaking with great pride and trying to impress people, especially about oneself. Boasting is annoying. If your love of someone is based on what they do or have, that is not love. Boasting is selfish and not a loving thing to do.

It's okay to talk about your significant other, friends, children or family members, about how they make you feel, or some of the things they have accomplished, when you aren't trying to impress others or be condescending. You can say those things with a cheerful heart and good intentions. If you want to boast about something, boast in the Lord.

> But God chose the foolish things of the world to shame the wise. He chose the weak things of the world to shame the strong. And God chose what the world thinks is not important—what the world hates and thinks is nothing. He chose these to destroy what the world thinks is important. God did this so that no one can stand before him and boast about anything. It is God who has made you part of Christ Jesus. And Christ has become for us wisdom from God. He is the reason we are right with God and pure enough to be in his presence. Christ is the one who set us free from sin. So, as the Scriptures say, "Whoever boasts should boast only about the Lord" (1 Corinthian 1:27-31, ERV)

3. Love is not dishonoring to others.

Look up the lyrics to the timeless song *Respect* sung by the late Aretha Franklin. Love is not disrespectful. To honor means to give someone respect and high consideration. Sadly, the song is asking for respect, when respect should be given freely in a relationship without having to ask. As you listen to or read the song lyrics, you recognize I'm sure that there is truth being stated. If respect/honor isn't given in a relationship, the dishonored person may have to withdraw. Being continually disrespectful in a relationship can break the other's spirit, close them off, and drive them away.

God commands us to respect others "Show respect for all people. Love your brothers and sisters in God's family. Respect God and honor the king" (1 Peters 2:17, ERV).

4. Love is not self-seeking.

It is not love when you are in a relationship just to lift you up or fulfill your needs. That is called lust, selfishness, and self-seeking. Love is not seeking its own benefit. It is a mutual thing. "In whatever you do, don't let selfishness or pride be your guide. Be humble, and honor others more than yourselves" (Philippians 2:3, ERV).

5. Love does not anger easily.

I used to have an issue with frustration and impatience in regards to my husband and children. It is something I have prayed about and worked on but I couldn't do it alone. Finding and praying the Scriptures that deal with anger has allowed God to help me control my anger. Meditating on those Scriptures has been the key.

Getting frustrated and impatient with my loved ones when it wasn't needed was slowly wounding the spirits of my husband and children. My emotions disobeyed how God wanted me to resolve issues. If I continued the impatience and frustration, they would eventually result in seriously hurt family members who would close themselves off to me and others.

I am not saying that we will never get angry with our loved ones. Love does not anger easily—*easily* being emphasized. That means taking the time to listen, hear their point of view, and remember that they are imperfect people (just like everyone else, including me). Now when I am angered, I take time alone to calm down before something is said that I may regret. I remind myself to show them mercy, to forgive and forget. I give the issue to God and give Him time and space to correct the problem—or adjust my attitude (or both).

Remember all the times Jesus showed you mercy and forgiveness and seek with God's help to do the same: "My dear brothers and sisters, take note of this: Everyone should be quick to listen, slow to speak and slow to become angry, because human anger does not produce the righteousness that God desires (James 1:19-20, NIV).

6. Love does not keep a record of wrongs.

I love writing lists. I still write grocery lists, to-do lists, and books-I-want-to-read lists. But I have never kept a list of things my husband, children, Mom, Dad, or any loved one did wrong to me.

I may remember a time or two I have been hurt, especially if the wound is fresh, but I don't linger on that hurt or offense. It is not healthy to keep a record of being wronged. Holding on will result in bitterness, stress, and mental and physical ailments that will affect your quality of life. Don't use the record as a chance to blackmail, or to bring guilt or shame to the one who hurt you. That is not love; that is evil.

No good can come from holding on to being wronged. Do not try to get revenge. It will backfire and fail. We are to forgive, show mercy and grace, and give the hurtful situation to God: "It is mine to avenge; I will repay. ... In due time their foot will slip; their day of disaster is near and their doom rushes upon them" (Deuteronomy 32:3, 5 NIV).

7. Love does not delight in evil.

Evil is not God's will and is the opposite of God's goodness. It has no place in any godly relationship. God doesn't like those who are evil: "Woe to those who call evil good and good evil, who put darkness for light and light for darkness, who put bitter for sweet and sweet for bitter" (Isaiah 5:20, NIV). Love doesn't intentionally harm. If you are being abused— physically, mentally, or spiritually—that is not love. Please get help for you and the abuser. Call the domestic violence hotline at 1-800-799-7233.

I pray you never experience evil from a loved one. Remember, there are red flags that can alert you to a person's character. If those red flags such as being easily angered, jealous, or controlling are visible, get out of that relationship unless your partner submits to counseling!

We all know that we are incapable of perfect love because we are imperfect people. However, we have just examined some of the things that love is not and will never have a part in. Although we may not always have that love feeling of butterflies in our stomach, and skies may not always be blue, love will never allow us to feel disrespected, shamed, guilt-ridden, or be the cause of physical pain or condemnation.

God is love. God is good. Love is good. Love does good.

Think About These Things

- Love is more than a feeling.
- Love is not negative.
- Love is not jealous.
- Love is not boastful or proud.
- Love is not self-seeking.
- Love does not anger easily.
- Love does not keep a record of wrongs.
- Love does not delight in evil.

You may wish to read about these things in the context of 1 Corinthians 13, which we will continue to examine in the next chapter

Chapter 3

The Thing Called Love . . .

What Love Is

If I have the gift of prophecy and can fathom all mysteries and all knowledge, and if I have a faith that can move mountains, but do not have love, I am nothing
(1 Corinthians 13:2, NIV).

First Corinthians 13 is known as the love chapter in the Bible. Paul started the chapter by describing various "good" characteristics and actions we can have and do, but if we don't do them with love, they don't really matter—or have the effect God intended. I reversed the order and looked at the things love is not in the previous chapter. In this chapter, let's look at its positive traits and results.

Love is powerful. Love seasons all of life and brings health to relationships, behaviors, and actions. Eighty-eight percent of Americans says love is a very important reason to get married according to the

"Eight Facts About Love and Marriage in America" article from the Pew Research Center. Love is a theme most often found in books, movies, and shows. Love is on everyone's mind, so let's explore the depths of love.

1. Love is patient.

Patience is one of the fruits of the Spirit. God is patient with us, and we need to exhibit that same patience with others. Being patient helps you experience God's goodness: "Always be humble and gentle. Be patient with each other, making allowance for each other's faults because of your love" (Ephesians 4:2). Having patience with our loved ones is important because it glorifies God and reveals His work in our lives.

"Now the God of patience and consolation grant you to be likeminded one toward another, according to Christ Jesus, that ye may with one mind and one mouth glorify God, even the Father of our Lord Jesus Christ" (Romans 15:5, KJV). Patience involves the calm endurance of a hardship, annoyance, inconvenience, delay, and the like according to *Oxford American Dictionary*. I love that definition.

The word *patience* comes from the Latin root word *patior*, which means to suffer.[2] God showed His love by sending His Son Jesus to suffer for us on the cross. That indicates that love involves suffering. Since love is patient, it makes patience a powerful source of peace and harmony in relationships. The suffering I'm referring to isn't by the hands of an abuser. That isn't the suffering God intends for us to experience, but godly suffering is described in the following manner:

If you are insulted because you bear the name of Christ, you will be blessed, for the glorious Spirit of God rests upon you. If you suffer, however, it must not be for murder, stealing, making trouble, or prying into other people's affairs. But it is no shame to suffer for being a Christian. Praise God for the privilege of being called by his name! . . . So if you are suffering in a manner that pleases God, keep on doing what is right, and trust your lives to the God who created you, for he will never fail you (1 Peter 4:14-16, 19).

2. Love is kind.

Kindness is another fruit of the Spirit and a descriptive word that applies to God and His ways: "Instead, be kind to each other, tenderhearted, forgiving one another, just as God through Christ has forgiven you" (Ephesians 4:32). Being kind is selfless. Kindness is defined as (do you see a pattern that I love definitions?) *gentle and considerate in one's manner or conduct towards others*. Although the word is an adjective, it is still an action word. It is what a person does that proves their kindness.

A relationship is not healthy when kindness is manifest only at the beginning, or is only one-sided. That is not love. Selfishness is being practiced and that relationship needs to change or end—quickly. In a healthy relationship, kindness is king. Kindness is displayed throughout the term of the relationship, not just at the beginning. Kindness is asking how your partner's day is going, even when you want to tell them all about yours first. Make his favorite meal, even though you don't like that type of food. Kindness doesn't have to be reciprocated but of course if a couple are trying to outdo one another in kindness, their relationship will be a heaven on earth.

Kindness is considerate which is based on understanding the other person. Everyone wants to be understood. Kindness is simple, but it's hard work. I advise you to express intentional kindness every opportunity you have.

3. Love never gives up.

In my childhood, my parents encouraged me to do my best in everything. What happened when I got a bad grade or didn't win a game? Did my parents stop loving me? No (I don't think they did). They encouraged me, gave me advice, and believed in me and my talents. Does God stop loving us when we sinned against him or did a stupid thing? No way. Nothing will ever separate us from the love of God through Christ Jesus:

> "For I am convinced that neither death nor life, neither angels nor demons, neither the present nor the future, nor any powers, neither height nor depth, nor anything else in all creation, will be able to separate us from the love of God that is in Christ Jesus our Lord (Romans 8:38-39, NIV).

A healthy relationship consists of encouraging, inspiring, empowering, disciplining, pushing, cheering, coaching, supporting, boosting, and offering reassuring words and actions towards your loved ones. Everyone benefits from a little boost of confidence from a loved one, no matter how "strong" they say they are. Love believes in you. Love doesn't give up on the person even if they give up on themselves.

My husband never gives up on me. He is my number one coach. He encourages me to do what God calls me to do—like writing this book. I do the same to him. We build each other up.

4. Love is hopeful and full of faith.

Hope is the feeling that what is wanted can be had or that events will turn out for the best, according to dictionary.com. Faith is confidence or trust in a person or thing, also from dictionary.com.

We live in a world where hope and faith seem to be in short supply. Many people have been acting in evil, corrupt ways toward others. Men and women doing those despicable actions and behaviors don't have love in their hearts. Their hope and faith are lost. Being hopeless is a terrible feeling; it leads to depression, anger, sadness, and other negative emotions. I know how hopelessness feels because of my experience years ago.

In 2006 after experiencing two years of infertility, my husband and I started going through the adoption process. We wanted to adopt a child from the foster system in our state. Excitement reigned in our little household. After completing the never-ending paperwork, interviews, background checks, and parenting classes, we got chosen to foster and then adopt a fifteen-month-old boy. We received the child profile sheet filled with his information and an adorable picture. Love exploded in our hearts for this little guy. A the time, he was living with a foster mom.

Ethan and I start to get ready for this little man. We talked to family and friends. About a week after receiving the profile sheet, I got a call from his caseworker who informed me the little guy's foster mom decided to adopt him. His adoption by his foster mom was wonderful! He didn't have to ride the emotional roller coaster of getting used to a new family. I was happy for him.

Little did I know how deeply this incident affected me. I cried after I got off the phone. I remember that day like it was yesterday. I was happy for him, yet sad for me. I worked that day on the evening shift as an assistant supervisor in the blood bank. I got to work but cried on and off so often that my manager told me to go home. Sadness filled my heart and mind. I couldn't eat. My stomach hurt. I couldn't sleep. I had weird obsessive thoughts of darkness. I cried constantly. I trembled periodically. My poor husband tried to comfort me to no avail. Back then he traveled for work and was gone for a few weeks.

I researched my symptoms online—not a good thing to do—and found out I was depressed. I called my doctor and told him my symptoms. He thought I simple had a bad case of PMS! He prescribed an anti-anxiety pill and another depression medicine for me. I didn't take the depression med, but took the anti-anxiety pill. The pill caused me to have no feelings. I hated it, so I stopped taking it.

Finally, I reached out to a therapist who really helped me. She explained the heartbreak of two years plus of infertility I experienced, then the hope of adopting our first child being destroyed. The situation was too much for my psyche and I experienced trauma. She said I had post-traumatic stress. Talking to the therapist about my feelings, thoughts, and emotions helped. I didn't take medicine. Knowing my diagnosis helped me and little by little, I started feeling better.

I had a relationship with Jesus during this time, but it wasn't as deep as it is now. However, I know He was with me. But because I was not then abiding in the power, the light, or the spiritual blessings from the heavenly realm I have in me through Jesus, I succumbed to the darkness this situation brought me. My sadness over this issue opened a gateway the enemy used to bind me! During the two months of this post-traumatic stress, I worked and never had an issue while working.

I experienced this hopelessness because I based my happiness and joy on something other than Jesus. I expected a child, this particular child, to be my ultimate source of fulfillment and to fill up the God-shaped hole in my heart. I'm not minimizing the longing to bear children. But I believed the lie that a child would make me complete. Jesus is my completion, my fulfillment. It took me many years after this incident to realize the truth. To finally believe the truth of how God feels about me, even after experiencing fifteen years of infertility. I am loved, worthy, significant, accepted, treasured, and more because God says so. Jesus dying on the cross is testament of God's love for me and you. God never lies. The Bible is truth.

Each of us will go through a time in our

lives when we hit rock bottom. Rock bottom may happen after we tried to do everything in our power and failed, or when someone hurt us. This down time may seem dark, bleak, and without hope. Rock bottom reveals how little control we have in life and points to God and His omniscience, wisdom, and love. We realize the only hope we have is in Christ Jesus and God is in control. When we die to ourselves, we truly live.

> Therefore, since we have been made right in God's sight by faith, we have peace with God because of what Jesus Christ our Lord has done for us. Because of our faith, Christ has brought us into this place of undeserved privilege where we now stand, and we confidently and joyfully look forward to sharing God's glory (Romans 5:1-2).
>
> Why am I discouraged? Why is my heart so sad? I will put my hope in God! I will praise him again—my Savior and my God! (Psalm 42:11).

There is good news. Faith in Jesus leads to joy! Hope in Jesus will never result in disappointment because we know how much God loves us. God will never fail or forsake those who love Him.

"Praise the Lord! He is good. God's love never fails. Praise the God of all gods. God's love never fails. Praise the Lord of lords. God's love never fails" (Psalms 136:1-3). Psalm 136 talks about God's unfailing love, please read it soon.

"And hope does not put us to shame, because God's love has been poured out into our hearts through the Holy Spirit, who has been given to us" (Romans 5:5, NIV). The Holy Spirit fills our hearts with love. Our faith and hope in Jesus permeate us with love. Spirit-filled love helps us excel in our relationships.

5. Love endures through every circumstance.

A few years ago, my goal was to run a 5K race. I have done aerobic exercises and strength training, but I was never a long-distance runner. Finishing a 5K would represent a tremendous accomplishment for me. I placed a picture of a woman running on my vision board for a constant visual reminder of my goal.

In October 2014, our whole family ran a 5K. I ran about 1.5 miles without stopping. My husband ran beside me, motivating and encouraging me to keep going. However, I couldn't run the whole 5K. I was happy that I accomplished my goal of completing the 5K. I knew I needed to build up endurance if I was going to run a 5K without stopping.

Fast forward to now and I still am trying to run three miles without stopping. I practice and push through the pain while saying Bible verses and prayers. I will keep practicing until I can run without stopping. Having endurance doesn't mean it won't hurt; it means I can take the pain and labored breathing of running a 5K.

"May the God who gives endurance and encouragement give you the same attitude of mind toward each other that Christ Jesus had" (Romans 15:5, NIV). True love will experience pain, hardship, and other difficulties but it will still be there holding us and our loved ones up. Love is strength; love gives strength. "And now these three remain: faith, hope and love. But the greatest of these is love" (1 Corinthians 13:13, NIV).

Think About These

- Love is much more than a feeling.
- Love is action; love gives.
- Love is a powerful thing.
- God is love.

Chapter 4

The Ultimate True Love

God showed how much he loved us by sending his one and only Son into the world so that we might have eternal life through him. This is real love—not that we loved God, but that he loved us and sent his Son as a sacrifice to take away our sins (1 John 4: 9-10 NLT).

The True Love Quiz

Directions: Read each question and answer yes or no. Give 2 points for every yes answer. Subtract 1 point for each no answer. Add and/or subtract points to find out if this is true love.

Is your loved one patient?

Is your loved one kind?

Is your loved one confident?

Is your loved one hopeful?

Does your loved one celebrate when truth and justice prevail?

Does your loved one encourage you?

Is your loved one considerate to you and others?

Does your loved one endure through every circumstance?

13-16 points – It's true love!

9-12 points – It's strong like leading to true love!

5-8 points – You need to rethink this relationship.

0-4 points – Definitely not true love. Toxic relationship. Break up now.

Although the quiz is not sophisticated, there is some truth in it. If you took the quiz and see that you answered many no's, you may be in an unhealthy relationship. A relationship that adds value to your life should be positive and life affirming, not negative and draining. A good relationship is healthy; if it's not healthy then it's not working the way God created relationships to work.

While working at a pregnancy resource center, I gave the true love quiz to many of my clients. We used colorful sheets of paper to keep the quizzes from being lost in their room so it wouldn't blend in with schoolwork or other papers. The following is how the interaction went when I presented the true love test to a client.

The client and I would be in a counseling room, decorated and furnished for comfort. I have just finished listening to her story. A thorough question-and-answer session helps me know more about her and how I can best help and serve her.

"Would you like to take a true love test?" I ask her.

"Sure."

I hand her over a brightly colored half sheet that has questions like these:

- Are they patient?
- Are they kind?
- Are they rude?

She takes it and while she is looking at it, I say, "Read it and for each question put your boyfriend's name in it."

She reads over it and sometimes she sees something, perhaps for the first time. Then I instruct her, "Go through it again but this time read it to yourself and put your name in there. Am I patient, etc.?"

She does it and I see it dawning on her again! That is when I stop her and ask, "Is it a healthy relationship when one is patient and the other isn't? How about kindness?" She shakes her head in the negative and sometimes a look of desperation, sadness, or anger wells up in her. Those emotions are to be expected, especially if the young woman has already bonded with the young man. I will be covering bonding in the chapter about hormones.

"Patient, kindness, not being jealous, boastful or rude are what true love is. These statements are guidelines and can be used for all your relationships: family, friends, boyfriends. This is the love Jesus has for you. Keep this paper in a special place." I ask if she would like to learn more and sometimes it's a yes and sometimes it's a no, but at that point, she knows that Jesus loves her.

Septembers in this southern town herald

the arrival of the county fair, a week or so of farm animals, fatty fair foods, and fun. The fair is a big deal. They even close school on Fridays for the fair. Because of the large attendance the fair is a prime place for outreach. The pregnancy resource center's booth had stickers, candy, facts about STD's, information about our services and the true love quiz. I will never forget the time I gave the quiz to a young man in his twenties.

After he read it over, he said, "Cool, where did you get this?"

"It's from the Bible," I said in a calm voice. "First Corinthians 13."

"Oh, thank you," he said with some trace of embarrassment, while putting the test in his pocket while walking away. I pray that he looked more into the Bible. Only God knows.

I've had people say to me after taking the true love test, "I wish I would have known this in my first marriage," or "I'm going to do this with my girlfriend/boyfriend." I've seen firsthand how many people really don't know what true love is, especially the true love Jesus has for them. I am passionate about one mission: to share Jesus' love in thought, word, and actions—which is one reason why I wrote this book you're reading right now.

When you believe and receive Jesus as your Lord and Savior along with His love for you, your life will be drastically changed forever in a good way. Believe that you are worthy of God's love because it's true! John 3:16 is a popular verse because it's a powerful proof of God's love. "God loved the people of this world so much that he gave his only Son, so that everyone who has faith in him will have eternal life and never really die. God did not send his Son into the world to condemn its people. He sent him to save them!" (John 3:16-17, CEV). Jesus' love is the ultimate true love.

The secret to true love is not a secret at all. Knowing and believing that God loves you, believing, trusting and obeying Jesus as your Lord and Savior will enhance your relationships. God is love; we love because He first loved us: "Dear friends, let us continue to love one another, for love comes from God. Anyone who loves is a child of God and knows God. But anyone who does not love does not know God, for God is love" (1 John 4:7-8).

It is hard to love if you don't know what love is. Don't believe TV shows, movies, books, social media, and other entertainment that depict love in an ungodly way. Love is more than hot, steamy sex, girls and guys locking in a passionate kiss, hip hop video vixens wearing sexy stuff, and other crude depictions. Those are examples of lust. Those feelings come and go quickly but don't endure, and the sexy bodies don't last very long.

As covered in chapter one, there is no specific timeline for falling in love. Ethan proposed to me ten months into our relationship. We married a year later and are going strong for 23 more. Although we have been married for 23 years, it wasn't always roses, chocolate, smiles, and puppy love. We have some amazing memories along with gut-wrenching heartaches—some out of our control (pregnancy losses) and others from stupid choices (divorce-worthy choices that I made). If we didn't have God in our lives along with caring friends and family, and if we had not given and received mercy, grace, and forgiveness from God and each other, we wouldn't have made it this far. Because my husband and I know, taste, and see God's love, it has expanded our capacity and desire to love one another. We ultimately need to know God's true love to give true love.

Don't be discouraged! I believe there is someone for everyone out there—including you. Knowing about God's love and what true love really is transforms and renews you into the person who deeply cherishes relationships. I am going to repeat this: believe that you are worthy of God's love. God cannot lie. He loved me and you and everyone else enough to send His Son to die for each one of us. Believe and trust it.

Think On These

- Read 1 John 4:7-20 about loving one another. What are your thoughts?
- Jesus' love is the ultimate true love.
- Believe that God loves you!

Chapter 5

Sex Uncovered

Lisa and Kevin have been together for six months. She thinks she is falling in love with him, but isn't sure. He is a sweet gentleman. He works, is childless, and lives on his own. Kevin grew up in a church but doesn't go often. Lisa grew up in church and still goes occasionally. She is growing in her relationship with God and accepted Jesus as her Savior, but is still not as strong as she would like to be. She would like to become more familiar with the Word of God and attend the young adult group her church has, but between college and work, she hasn't had much time.

God understands. He forgives me, she often thinks. But there is a little tug in her heart that she ignores. She and Kevin have been getting close but haven't had sex. Lisa is still a virgin, but she's been feeling some kind of way towards Kevin.

"Is he the one?" she wonders.

Her friends always remind her Kevin is a good catch. "Kevin is hot, Lisa!" adding fuel to the slow simmer she feels when Kevin is nearby. Kevin is a gentleman and hasn't pressured her for sex. They've kissed and hugged a few times, but it's never gone further.

Lisa forgot what she learned in her high school health class about sex. Sex was rarely talked about at her church. Her mom talked about it with her when she was young. Mom said to wait until marriage, but never gave a reason why.

Sex is everywhere! Lisa sees it in her favorite shows, vids, memes, and on IG and snapchat. When she does have time to read, she dives into those short romance novels that include a few heavy sex scenes, and that usually has her feeling aroused.

This Saturday, Kevin is taking her to her favorite restaurant, and then they're going to see a new romantic comedy movie that everyone is raving about. *Kevin is so good to me. I'm thinking about maybe giving him a little present of my own*, Lisa thinks. She is still a little nervous knowing this is a big decision. She calls her friends and tells them her thoughts about Saturday.

"Girl, about time!" One of them said.

"Are you sure, Lisa? Sex is such a big step. I don't want you to get hurt," the other said.

"Don't do it, Lisa. Do you know how God feels about sex before marriage? There's so much more to sex than what they show on TV," said her voice-of-reason friend (everyone has a voice-of-reason friend).

OMG! I'm so confused. I know God wants me to wait, but I really don't know why. Sex is what people do when they're in love. Well, that's what I've been told. I think I'm in love with Kevin. Sex might be the thing that will let me know. Her thoughts run rampant.

They say to follow your heart, so okay. Saturday

is it. Yup, I got to get a cute outfit! Lisa concludes. She continues to experience a little tug of hesitation and doubt in her heart, especially when she thinks about having sex with Kevin. She's not sure what she should do with that tug.

Saturday night arrives. Lisa is looking extra cute in her new outfit and shoes.

"Wow Lisa, you look beautiful," Kevin says. Dinner was enjoyable. The movie demanded their tears and laughter. It was the "perfect" evening.

Yup, tonight is the night, Lisa thinks to herself as Kevin lets her into his apartment.

Butterflies invade her stomach. The words of her mom, friends, and people at church begin to flood her mind. She is confused about sex. *But it's my life*, she reasons to herself, as she takes her coat off and lays it on the chair in the living space. The tug in her heart makes her jump a little.

"You good?" Kevin asks as he walks beckoning her to fall into his arms.

"I'm good," she says quietly, as he wraps his arms around her. She trembles a little and he lets go. He takes her hand and guides her over to the couch.

"I had fun tonight, Lisa. I've been thinking," he says with a look in his eyes as they sit down.

Oh no! I think I know what he is going to say!

"I've been thinking too, Kevin," she says with fake confidence.

I don't know if I'm ready, Lisa thinks nervously to herself.

Have you ever found yourself in a predicament like the one Lisa is in? Do you struggle with some of those same feelings? What decision did you make? How did it make you feel?

Perhaps you are in a relationship right now that has you feeling like Lisa. Maybe you desire to have more information about sex, to make a good choice about whether to engage in it. If you have been given information about sex, it's essential that you know what God's Word says, and for you to know how your body responds to sex.

Be mindful of the source of information. Where does it come from? Is it truth? Is it in line with God's word? Not everything you hear is accurate and true, especially from what the mainstream media teaches or portrays about sex. There is incomplete information, hearsay, opinion, and/or lies about sex that are prevalent in modern culture. These can skew your thinking and judgment, and damage you spiritually and physically if you believe and act on them. There is biblical and biological truth about sex concerning the way God designed it to function. When the truth about God's design for sex is known and understood, I promise it all make sense! Let me tell you more.

Sex Defined

Sex is defined as any intimate activity between two people that involves arousal, stimulation, and/or a response by at least one of them. That means kissing with the intent to have sex, touching each other's private parts, watching porn, reading erotica, sexting (sending erotic text messages), sending and receiving nude pictures, showering or bathing together, sitting on his lap, self-touch to get aroused, oral sex, using sex toys, etc. Anything that is done with the purpose to make you "feel good," up to and including orgasm.

As mentioned in the short story about Lisa,

sex is everywhere. The way people perceive sex has changed in our culture since the sexual revolution of the '60s. Slowly but surely, we've gotten away from God's view and design for sex—that it is saved to be experienced between a husband and wife. The following survey results are an example of how these views have changed.

In a Barna Group survey, they asked participants their opinions on traditional Christian sexual ethics: *Traditional Christian sexual ethics* teaches that sex should only be within a marriage between a man and woman. The results are below (www.Barna.org):

> 53% of *practicing Christians* said this view was moral.
>
> 36% of people with *no faith* said it was unrealistic.
>
> 28% of those of *other faith* said it was moral.[1]

As you see there are different and surprising views. What really stood out to me was those with no faith didn't even vote for it being moral.

The word *moral* is seldom found in our culture today. With the word *relativism* being the prevailing belief, most people think there are no absolutes. Saying there are no absolute truths is a contradiction. There is absolute truth: God and His Word.

The *Oxford American Dictionary* defines moral as: 1) concerned with the goodness and badness of human character or with the principles of what is right or wrong in conduct; 2) virtuous (goodness); 3) capable of understanding and living by the rules of morality; and 4) based on people's sense of what is right or just.

To summarize, "moral" means doing what is right. Understanding what is right and wrong gives us a sense of boundaries, and boundaries are what we need. We teach children what is right and wrong for their safety and the safety of others. The same need for teaching those same principles apply to teens, young adults, and older adults too!

When there are no boundaries, chaos prevails, and our world is in chaos today. Evidence from the sexualization of everything includes the hurt, grief, selfishness, violence, and hopelessness that are found everywhere in the lives of Christians and non-believers alike.

This Barna survey referred to above had a second part. Results from part two of the survey revealed that more people are viewing sex as a form of *self-fulfillment* and *pleasure* for themselves. In other words, people are having sex for selfish reasons. With that perspective, they are missing out on what sex truly is. God's plan for sex is not self-centered. Those who don't understand or believe that are missing out on unbelievable sex with their future spouse! God knows what He is doing. More on this later.

I understand why 36% of those with *no faith* believe that saving sex for marriage is unrealistic. It's likely because they are inundated with sex on TV shows, commercials, movies, social media, internet, books (especially erotica), clothing, magazines, music, and apps. The more someone is bombarded with sex, the more difficult it is to think of sex as something special. They are blinded to the truth of God and deceived by this world.

It is dangerous out here these days. As a married woman, I too must be careful as to what I'm watching or reading. No one is immune to the sex saturation. I must intentionally monitor what I listen to, watch, or read because certain things can cause me to entertain thoughts that may feel good for a minute but in the end, make me feel bad and convicted. I will share more about guarding your eyes, ears, heart and mind in Chapter Three. For now, let me simply mention this one verse: "Above all else, guard your heart, for everything you do flows from it" (Proverbs 4:23, NIV).

God's Truth

If you're waiting to have sex until you're married, I applaud you for that decision. You're obeying God and His design for sex and He is pleased with you. As you continue reading, you'll understand how sex is more than a physical connection; sex involves the brain along you're your body, mind, and soul.

If you have had sex out of order, you're not doomed to the fiery pit of hell, and you can indeed restart your purity journey. I don't want to alienate you or cause you to experience shame (a lie of the enemy) because of the choices you made. At the same time, I don't want you to think that it's permissible for you to continue to engage in non-marital sexual activity. I simply want you to know the truth about repentance and God's forgiveness. I speak the truth as best I can in love because you are God's creation and you need to hear it. You are precious to Him. He loves you and knows what's best for you. Premarital or extra-marital sex is not in your best interests—no matter how you try to talk yourself into the fact that it is.

God wants what is best for you and that is

waiting to have sex with your husband (or wife for any men who are reading). Knowing this truth shall set you free: "Then you will know the truth, and the truth will set you free" John 8:32 (NIV). You will be free from anxiety, doubt, worry, and pain when you choose to wait.

Think On These

- Sex is defined as any intimate activity between two people that involves arousal, stimulation, and/or a response by at least one party.
- Moral means having a sense of right and wrong as God defines it.
- You need boundaries that will give you the confidence to say no.
- There is hope.
- God loves you.
- The truth shall set you free!

Dear Lord,

I pray that You open Your daughter's heart and mind to the truth of Your love for her. I pray that she is receptive to the truth of sex, it's consequences, and why You made sex to be saved for marriage between husband and wife. I pray she finds confidence and power in herself to make the right choices to live the life of purpose You have for her. Thank You, Lord, for giving me this opportunity to share Your truth and love with Your precious daughter. In Jesus' name I pray, amen.

Chapter 6

Your Period . . .

The Menstrual Cycle

Explained

"Whenever a woman has her menstrual period, she will be ceremonially unclean for seven days. Anyone who touches her during that time will be unclean until evening" (Leviticus 15:19).

Have you tried to read the book of Leviticus, the third book of the Bible in the Old Testament? When I took classes for my master's degree in public health, we discussed how the book of Leviticus contains public health principles, especially the laws about contagious skin diseases and treatment of contaminated clothing through proper washing.

I remember when my mother talked to me about menstruation during the summer going into sixth grade. As we were sitting in my bedroom, I was uncomfortable and not really paying attention. I remember the setting but not too much of what she said. When I started my period, a discharge soiled my underwear. I wondered what the heck it was. It took about two days for what my mom told me about menstruation to make sense to me! To this day I still don't remember what made me realize I had started my period. But I do remember where I told her. Our family was trying to play tennis at our local YMCA and I told her while we were out on the court. She was excited; I was mortified!

Fast forward now and I think, *Ugh, these cramps. Just be done, period!*

When I worked at the Pregnancy Resource Center ministry, I realized how many women didn't understand their menstrual cycle and the reproductive process. Many do not know how ovulation, conception, and sex work together. I'm including this in the book because the menstrual cycle is an important part of being a woman and it plays a big part in sexual intercourse. One of the reasons for sexual intercourse is to pro-create, male and female joining together to create new life—babies and children.

One of the distinct characteristics that God designed females for is the ability to bear children. The complex processes a woman's body goes through every month is all labeled the *menstruation cycle*. This cycle involves getting an egg ready to be fertilized and making a woman's body ready to carry a baby if conception occurs. The menstrual cycle has three phases:

1. The Follicular Phase. It starts the first day of menstrual bleeding, otherwise known as a "period."

In the follicular phase, the follicles found in the ovaries contain the eggs which have starting to develop for ovulation. This is done by the follicle-stimulating hormone (FSH). During this phase, if the hormones estrogen and progesterone are low, and conception (pregnancy) hasn't occurred, the uterus will shed its lining, causing bleeding, thus the "period."

2. The Ovulatory Phase. Ovulation is the release of an egg (or eggs) from the ovary. When the luteinizing hormone (LH) rises, about 10 to 12 hours later an egg will be released from an ovary (or ovaries). The egg is picked up by a fallopian tube and starts moving down to the uterus. This is also when conception can happen if the egg encounters and is penetrated or fertilized by any present sperm. During this phase, an egg-white colored mucus discharge may be noticed when wiping after using the restroom; it may also appear as a "wet" spot on underwear. This mucus helps the sperm survive, potentially keeping it vital for 16 to 32 hours. The days before ovulation and the day of ovulation itself are referred to as "fertile" days. These are the days when pregnancy can occur. It is important to know that pregnancy may occur *whenever* sexual intercourse is performed and sperm was released! That is one of the main reasons for sexual intercourse.

The number of days in these first two phases together can vary. It is not true that everyone ovulates on the 14th day of their cycle, or that everyone's cycle length is 28 days. Every woman is different. That's what it's helpful to keep a calendar of your monthly cycle.

3. The Luteal Phase. This starts after ovulation and usually lasts consistently for 14 days, unless

the woman is pregnant. The ruptured follicle closes after releasing the egg and a corpus luteum forms, producing the hormone progesterone. Estrogen is present during this phase. Both these hormones help to thicken the lining of the uterus to get it ready for a baby if conception occurs. If conception doesn't occur, the corpus luteum disintegrates, progesterone and estrogen lower, and the thickened uterus lining starts to shed (the period). Then, the cycle begins again.

A woman's menstrual cycle is usually the same number of days, varying from 23 to 32 days. It can change when she is stressed either physically or mentally. If you have any questions, problems, or concerns with your menstrual cycle, please talk to a trusted healthcare provider. Don't be afraid to ask questions. Taking charge of your health begins with you.

Think on These:

- A distinct characteristic of a woman is being able to bear children.
- The process a woman's body goes through every month to release the egg and get ready for a baby is called the menstruation cycle.
- There are three phases in the cycle.
- One of the main reasons for sexual intercourse is to make babies.
- You *can* get pregnant whenever you have sexual intercourse.

Chapter 7

Your Brain On Sex

"Oh, let me warn you, sisters in Jerusalem, by the gazelles, yes, by all the wild deer: Don't excite love, don't stir it up, until the time is ripe—and you're ready" (Song of Songs 2:7, MSG).

In the Song of Songs, this verse is repeated twice for a reason: a warning not to initiate sexual activity until "you're ready." We have seen so far that part of that readiness is marriage, and again and again I have seen the results of people ignoring this advice in the center where I have been a counselor. Let me share one story with you.

I once counseled what unbeknownst to me would be an unforgettable client. She had a child, a history of two abortions she was trying to recover from (pregnant by the same young man), and thought she might be pregnant again. She was distraught. She didn't want to be pregnant, but she didn't want to go through another abortion. She and the young man weren't together. She loved him but he would only use her for sex. She knew how he felt about her but she struggled to resist him, even though she knew he was not good for her. She was sad, hurt, and confused.

I empathized with her story and expressed my sympathy. I could feel her sorrow and pain. The reason she felt this way for him was because she had bonded with him because they had engaged in sexual intercourse. The bond grew stronger the more she was with him, making it harder for her to leave him. She ignored the advice in the Song of Solomon again and again, and the agony and heartbreak were inescapable. She wasn't ready. Read on to understand why she was having such trouble separating herself from this young man who had impregnated her on numerous occasions.

The Brain

There was an anti-drug commercial on TV in the early 1990s. In it, a hand held an egg and the narrator said, "This is your brain." Then the hand cracked the egg over a hot frying pan. As the egg started to sizzle and cook, the voice said, "This is your brain on drugs." It was a simple commercial with a powerful message: When you use drugs, they fry your brain. We have seen the truth of this again and again. Recently, rise of opioid addiction and its effects have been well documented by the media and prove the message of the egg-and-skillet public service announcement.

Though sex may not have as devastating an effect as drugs (but can), sex has similar effects on our brain. Our brain gets fired up and changes when we have sex. Sex is addicting for a reason and it's this.

Our brains are another sex organ. There is more to sex than the physical act; there is a mental and emotional part as well.

The brain works like a powerful computer. It processes information that it receives from the senses and body and returns messages back to the body. The brain and the spinal cord are part of the central nervous system. Brain tissue is made up of about 100 billion nerve cells (neurons) and one trillion supporting cells which stabilize the tissue.[1]

Our brain has many jobs to perform, like keeping our hearts beating and our lungs breathing. It sends information to various organs to digest food, urinate, and/or have sexual responses. All these jobs are autonomic; they are involuntary and work without us telling them to. This is called the Autonomic Nervous System (ANS). The ANS receives information about the body and its environment, which stimulates cells to do their job.

The ANS is not the same as our mind. It doesn't make judgements, it doesn't know right from wrong. It has no morals or values (this is important, so I will repeat this many times). Its main job is to keep our body processes running smoothly to help us stay alive and procreate.

Our brain has two sides and many parts. The *left cerebral cortex* is responsible for speech and language. The *right cerebral cortex* supplies spatial information, such as where your foot is now. The *thalamus* provides the cerebrum with sensory information from the skin, eyes, and ears, as well as other information. The *hypothalamus* regulates hunger, thirst, and sleep. Together with the pituitary gland, the hypothalamus also regulates the hormones in your body.[1]

Hormones are chemical messengers sent through the bloodstream to various parts of the body so they can function properly. Neurotransmitters are chemical messengers conveyed via the nervous system. Oxytocin and vasopressin are amazing because they can act as hormones and neurotransmitters. They have roles to play in sexual desires and behaviors.

The Brain on Sex: Dopamine Makes You Feel Dope

Dopamine is a neurotransmitter associated with movement, attention, learning, and the brain's pleasure-and-reward system.[2] It makes you feel dope when you do something good, exciting, and pleasurable, like eating chocolate. But it can also make you feel good when doing risky, dangerous, or immoral things.

Dopamine is believed to play a leading role in the motivation-and-reward process. "Motivation refers to an internal drive to engage in a specific behavior, typically in pursuit of a reward or reinforcer. This can refer to natural reward seeking behaviors, such as those directed towards obtaining food and water, sex, or social interaction, as well as learned behaviors, including behaviors involved in drug seeking and taking."[3]

Dopamine activity is at its highest levels during adolescence and emerging adulthood.[4] Dopamine rewards drug use such as cigarette smoking, marijuana, and heroin. It also rewards pre-marital sex, porn, fast driving, and other things that are harmful. What's not good is that the dope feeling we can get from the dopamine reward can cause us to increase dangerous behaviors so we can keep achieving that dope feeling. Dopamine can cause us to make unwise sexual choices that can have devastating consequences.

Dopamine doesn't have any morals; it's simply doing its job. It is involuntary and can't tell right from wrong or good or bad. It clouds our judgment. It rewards all types of behaviors, both good and bad. Dopamine works in a positive way for married couples. The husband and wife actually become addicted to each other.[4] This helps them bond and stay together.

Dopamine isn't "bad." This neurotransmitter motivates and assists us for learning, romance, reproduction, and most important of all, God. I believe dopamine's primary purpose is to propel us to experience God and His word daily and experience the rush that only God gives. Knowing and using God's wisdom produces the surge of dopamine that comes from making a wise decision, an addiction that is healthy and satisfying. We are made to crave and serve God.

Oxytocin, The Bonder

Oxytocin is a bonding hormone and neurotransmitter. Found in men and women, it's more active in females.[5] The female sex hormone estrogen reinforces the influence of oxytocin (oxytocin book).[6] Oxytocin is released during sexual intercourse, intimate/sexual touching with another person, at the onset of labor, and nipple stimulation after delivery of an infant.[7]

Let's focus for a minute on the role of oxytocin in sexual intercourse and intimate/sexual touching. The role of oxytocin is to create bonding and trust in other people. It increases the desire for more touch and causes bonding of the woman to the man she has been spending time and is in physical contact with.[4] The touching can lead to sexual intercourse.

During sexual intercourse and orgasm, oxytocin floods the brain, causing a woman to desire this repeatedly with the man she has bonded to, causing the bond to grow stronger.[8] This bonding can result in a long-term relationship and this bond is an actual, real physical bond—invisible to the eye but a real connection nonetheless. The cells of the people bonded are connected through a chemical reaction. When the two break up, it physically hurts and can cause sadness, depression, withdrawal, anxiety, insomnia, loss of appetite, low concentration, and other signs of grief.[9] The longer the relationship has existed, the deeper the hurt from the bond breaking. Women are affected more than men. We are fine china, ladies—easily wounded and broken.

Just like dopamine, oxytocin has no morals or logic. It's just doing its job and it will do it with whomever you are intimate. It clouds your judgement, making it hard to think logically where the other person is concerned. Bonding starts with the first sexual encounter, which means there is no such thing as a casual hook-up. A hook-up starts the bonding. One-night stands lead to bonding. "Friend" sex leads to bonding. Casual sex causes pain and you can see that multiple partners leads to all kinds of confusion and problems.

Oxytocin causes a woman to trust someone she touches and has a lot of contact with. Remember oxytocin doesn't care what type of man he is. It can get harder and harder for a woman, especially a younger one, to say no. A 20-second hug can cause the hormone to flood their brain, starting the trust and bonding process![10]

Constant hooking up, having sex, and breaking up can cause difficulties bonding in the future. It causes the brain to form a pattern and accepts having sex and breaking up with someone as normal. Constant hook-ups and break-ups make it harder to form lasting relationships.[11] A hardened heart is formed, making those things that God designed, a healthy marriage, and great sex within that marriage, just a dream. Not all is lost. A long-term, healthy relationship can be a reality through prayer, professional help, personal growth, and trust in God.

This One is For Men

I wrote this book for women but I'm hoping a woman will read parts of it to their man. I'm hoping she will either have him read or read to him this section. Women are not the only one with hormones and chemicals involved in family and intimacy matters. Something called **vasopressin** is a neurotransmitter that helps the man bond to a woman and his children. Vasopressin and oxytocin are "sister" hormones and sometimes work in tandem. It

- Instills courage and eliminates the feeling of danger
- Promotes anxiety—heightens senses for the surroundings
- Increases and leads to aggression against intruders (a protective measure seen in

the lab with male rats and protecting their offspring)
- Facilitates in social bonding, especially in males[12]

Just like the other two neurotransmitters, vasopressin doesn't have any morals. It does its job no matter who the man sleeps with. Clouding his judgment, it can cause a bond to form with a toxic woman who is not good for him. A man, just like a woman, must think and choose wisely before he makes the decision to have sex with a woman.

If a man has serial relationships and/or has sex with multiple women, he too will lessen the ability to bond and make it harder to stay in a long-term relationship. Both oxytocin and vasopressin increase levels of dopamine, in turn making a strong bond.[13]

Our Mind

The characteristics of dopamine, oxytocin, and vasopressin were discovered in large part through scientific experiments with non-human mammals. Research performed on humans has limits because of ethics. Results from brain research of non-human mammals is used because of the similarity of the hormones' and neurotransmitters' functions. But there is a big difference between humans and animals.

Humans think, choose, and feel. We have a mind. We have the ability for self-control over urges and other animal-like behavior. God designed us to have authority over animals. We have the power of choice. God created humans in His image. We are His masterpiece, unique and perfectly crafted. To say we are nothing but animals is dishonors God and is contrary to God's word. It's important stand in that truth of identity that God says we have. God made us each unique and that is expressed in our thinking, feeling, and choices.

Isn't it awesome how God designed hormones and neurotransmitters to work? There is a reason why they are designed to work that way. When used correctly, these neurotransmitters and hormones bond the husband and wife to help them stay together and raise their children. Healthy married parents have a positive impact on the children's lives.

Children who are raised in a two-parent home have a better quality of life because both parents are needed to enrich their children's lives. God created women and men to complement each other; they have different qualities that children need. Now you see what sex is so much more than a physical act. It is a holistic act that includes the body, brain, mind, and soul. When we obey God in His design for sex, it will result in freedom and joy.

Things to Think About

- The brain is a powerful part of sex.
- Three neurotransmitters (hormones) work with our sexual desires and behaviors.
- Dopamine makes us feel dope when we do something exciting, risky, pleasurable, or intense.
- Oxytocin is for bonding, trust, and attachment. It is more active in women.
- Vasopressin helps a man to bond to a woman and his children.
- All three of these hormones have no morals. They do not think wisely and cause bonding no matter what type of person we have sex with.
- Break-ups literally hurt because the chemical bond you have with the other person is broken.
- Hugging a man for 20 seconds starts the bonding process—be careful who you hug!
- Having serial relationships with sex, and bonding and breaks-ups cause the brain to think its normal, thus making it more difficult to bond and have long, healthy relationships.
- God designed sex between a husband and wife to procreate and become one, and as a form of worship.
- Sex is wonderful when done the way God designed it.

Dear Lord,

I pray the knowledge and understanding of the intricate workings of sex and Your wonderful design for it helps me grasp the truth and counters all the lies and half-truths I have believed. I pray You continue to help me realize how sex is more than a physical act. It's a gift from You that is emotional, physical, and spiritual and to be shared with my husband. I pray I keep the importance of waiting for my husband uppermost in my mind and heart. I pray that You free me from all the consequences that sexual sin such as pre-marital sex can bring. I pray I focus more on my value, purpose, and calling You have for me in Your Kingdom. In Jesus' name I pray, amen.

Chapter 8

Eight Reasons Why You May Get It on Before Marriage

Yet God has made everything beautiful for its own time. He has planted eternity in the human heart, but even so, people cannot see the whole scope of God's work from beginning to end (Ecclesiastes 3:11).

Let me be clear, sex is great and is a part of God's design for us. Awareness of our sexuality is normal. However, we must be aware of what we can do with that sexuality, for it can be a tremendous of blessing or heartache. Is it honoring God and ourselves? Is how we are expressing our sexuality how we want to be identified? Is it controlling our lives or are we controlling it?

From my years of experience working at a women's ministry, I learned and understood the various reasons many of these women had sex before the time was right. Most issues, problems, attitudes, and reactions have a root cause—a reason why those things are happening. These issues, problems, attitudes, and reactions are simply the manifestation of that root cause, so knowing and confronting that cause is important if we are to be the sexual beings that God intended instead of the one the world informed.

Reason 1: Searching for love

Many girls believe that having sex with their boyfriends will result in the boyfriend loving them. Boys may pressure the girls to have sex, saying that having sex is a way to prove their love. However, real love doesn't pressure you for sex. It's important that you distinguish the difference between love and lust. Love is selfless and giving as we discussed earlier. Lust is selfish and takes. For a refresher, re-read the previous chapters that describe what love is and what love isn't.

Love is a basic human need and motivator. There are theories that have been devised as to the reason for our love need. If love isn't realized, especially the love of a father in one's life, a person will continue to seek that love and fulfill this need by any possible means—sometimes by doing things that are not consistent with their values or beliefs.

God knows of this need you have for love. He is the one who created you with it. He knows the importance of a father's and mother's unconditional love for their children. If and when you have children, please hug them and let them know they are loved unconditionally, not just with words but show them by your actions. Remember, God loves all His creation but especially loves His new creation through Christ with an eternal love. His love is the ultimate love. When you search for love outside of God's will, you open yourself up to all kinds of problems—as we have discussed to this point.

Reason 2: Not knowing your identity

Sadly, our culture portrays women as sex symbols and objects. Some young women accept this label, so they think dressing in a sexy, revealing manner will get them the attention required that will lead to love. It's true, wearing provocative apparel draws attention, but it's lust attention and not love. Those women may feel they need to be good at something to find a partner and think sex is all they are good at—or all they need to be good at to attract and keep a man. Others are curious about their sexuality and experiment, but later find they were playing with fire and got burned.

Sisters, our identity is not based on sex or sexuality!

Our identity is based on different character traits, our likes and dislikes, and our innate, God-given gifts. God created each of us with unique thought patterns. No one thinks the same way. These qualities and tendencies emerge during different seasons as you go through life. It is what makes you unique. God made only one of you for a divine purpose and your uniqueness depends not on your conformity to the world's standards, but on preserving your God-given individuality.

Our identity can also come from an occupation or another type of label we associate ourselves with, like a hairstylist, a basketball player, a wife, a girlfriend, a baker, a boss lady, a model, etc. These identifiers or roles can change, so you shouldn't let your world or self-worth revolve around them. There is only one identifying label that has a firm, lasting foundation and that is to be found in Christ Jesus. If and when you believe that the Lord and Savior Jesus Christ died for your sins and rose again to the right hand of God the Father, you become an heir to the Kingdom and all God's promises for good!

> But when the right time came, God sent his Son, born of a woman, subject to the law. God sent him to buy freedom for us who were slaves to the law, so that he could adopt us as his very own children. And because we are his children, God has sent the Spirit of his Son into our hearts, prompting us to call out, "Abba, Father." Now you are no longer a slave but God's own child. And since you are his child, God has made you his heir (Galatians 4:4).

Princesses aren't only found in Europe. When we are in Christ, we are royalty! When you are in Christ, you are royalty!

Reason 3: Ignorance where sex is concerned

The physical part of sex is what's always talked about, examined, and glorified. However, many people overlook the emotional and spiritual aspects of sex, which are rarely talked about. Parents teach untruths about sex to their children because they themselves aren't armed with the truth.

I ran a survey on my website and one of the questions was: What were you taught about sex? Here are some answers:

- "I was taught that sex can cause a lot of diseases, but it is very nice."
- "Not much."
- "Sex after marriage!"
- "At home the topic was avoided *completely*."
- "You'll know when the time is right."

The last was from a woman I spoke with in person. She asked me, "What was that supposed to mean? I didn't know when the time is right."

One of my saddest counseling memories is of a 13-year-old who had sex with a boy the same day she met him. She didn't know his name or anything about him, but unfortunately, became pregnant. Although she did have a lot of other issues in her life, she didn't have a clue about the emotional, spiritual, or physical aspects of sex.

We have heard the saying, "the truth shall set you free," which are Jesus' words found in John 8:32. We must arm ourselves with truth and facts about everything—who God is, who Jesus is, who we are, who you are. You get the truth by reading the Bible, and praying for wisdom, understanding, and knowledge. You should read other books, attend webinars, go to conferences, talk with experts, and attend a good church that teaches biblical truth. When we know the truth about things, especially things or actions that can have harsh consequences, we are enabled to make better choices. And of course, my advice in the context of this book is to learn the truth about sex and God's intentions for it.

Reason 4: Loneliness

It is possible to be with someone physically and still feel lonely. Remember, your bonding hormones have no morals so you can hook-up and bond with someone who is toxic or who has no intention of having any kind of relationship with you except sexual. Then you sit at home yearning for them, while you are out of sight and out of mind with them. When a relationship ends, you can feel worse because of the effects of the broken bond that we discussed earlier.

This goes back to who you are in a relationship with. You want to be with people who will help you thrive, not people who will suck the life out of you. It is better to be single, healthy, and happy than to be in a toxic relationship that leaves you stressed and sad—and lonely even though you are with someone. God made us to be in relationship with others to have friends, not just boyfriends. Here are some simple tips for how to combat loneliness that don't involve sex:

1. Call and/or hang out with friends.
2. Join a small group at church.
3. Volunteer at an organization whose mission you identify with.
4. Try something different to meet new people.
5. Join a sports league or travel club, or

sign up for a class at your local library or community college.
6. Visit a park.
7. Find a hobby that involves others like pottery or singing in a community choir.
8. Call and visit your family.
9. Be personable when you meet new friends..
10. Pray for God to give you ideas for the places where you can meet new people.

Remember you are never alone. God is always with you, but He created you to be with others. Don't isolate yourself, and don't use sex as a way to meet new friends!

Reason 5: Vulnerable immaturity

Teen and adolescent brains are still developing. They are fragile and having sex before reaching a certain level of maturity can have long-term, negative consequences. Depression, regret, and sexual addiction are some examples.[14] Suicide can also be a result of creating a life mess for which there is no easy escape or answer.

The brain's prefrontal cortex—the part that helps with values and judgement—matures around the age of 20. Our primal limbic system and increased dopamine receptors raise the chance of gambling with risky sexual behaviors. Emotions and physical drives that are not properly managed can tip the scales away from logical or wise choices concerning sexual activity. This is increased or pronounced following previous sexual activity.

Some girls may be coerced into having sex if a boy or man is always touching them, i.e., holding their hands, giving back rubs, hugs, or light touches on the arms. Those touches activate the oxytocin and cause her to "trust" him.

Ladies, I remind you: We are made like fine china—beautiful but easily broken. It is easy for our brains to "trust" a man, even though he may not be the right one for us. That's because oxytocin is doing its job. We need to use discernment and wisdom regarding whom we let touch or hug us. Pray for discernment and wisdom; listen to the Spirit. And help protect our younger sisters who are not ready for the responsibilities or ramifications of premarital sex.

Reason 6: The culture

Sex is everywhere. Almost every TV show, movie, book, and song alludes to sex. Our current culture strives to convince us that its permissible to have sex whenever we wish, with anyone we choose, to do what makes us happy. The motto of this philosophy is YOLO (You Only Live Once). Life is a party. But in reality, and on the inside, people are lonely, hurt, and confused and doing exclusively what makes us happy can make us sad and depressed.

Culture is a collection beliefs, opinions, thinking, and/or customs of a group of people or society. However, what culture believes or does isn't always truth or right, and isn't shaped and guided by good morals. Cultural values are a strong force that seeks to have its subjects conform, and many follow them out of ignorance or uncertainty.

There is a psychological impact of influence is called social proof, which is "one means we use to determine what is correct is to find out what other people think is correct."[2] Many people use social proof when deciding appropriate or acceptable behavior. This principle can be good in some instances, It can also lead people astray when people assume something is correct behavior is when in truth it is incorrect or harmful.

The principle of social proof takes over when people are mindless and reactive with their behaviors, when they don't think about the action/behavior and just do it. This is animal-like and foolish thinking (or non-thinking). God made humans above the animals, and He says a lot about fools in the Bible.

> A single rebuke does more for a person of understanding than a hundred lashes on the back of a fool (Proverbs 17:10).

> It is senseless to pay to educate a fool, since he has no heart for learning (Proverbs 17:16).

> Fools care nothing for thoughtful discourse; all they do is run off at the mouth (Proverbs 18:2, MSG).

God created you to think, feel, and choose. Take time and think before you decide. Take an extra minute or two and think about why you want to engage in a certain action or behavior. Ask some questions: Is it because everyone is doing it? Is it truth? Is it what God wants me to do? Will it harm others or me, if not now, then in the future? Is it God-honoring?

Don't be a fool.

Reason 7: Environment

There is a culture of the society in which we live, but then there are sub-cultures where you work or live, worship, or go to school. The environment you live in influences your behaviors and actions. The biggest influencers are your parents and family, followed by schools and neighborhoods. How your parents solved problems or reacted to situations influence your behaviors. Take a moment to think about how you solve problems. Are there any similarities to anyone you were close to? Who are you acting or reacting like? Is it healthy or toxic?

The workplace, your friends, schools, and social media are included in your sphere of influence. Awareness of the events in your environment must be a constant activity. Put space between yourself and toxic environments. Guard your hearts from negative pressure and subtle influences in your surroundings. Although your environment can affect you, it shouldn't have power over your actions. You have power over your own actions and choices if you are conscious of what they are and why you are doing them. Every action starts with a thought.

> For God has not given us a spirit of fear and timidity, but of power, love, and self-discipline (2 Timothy 1:7).

Reason 8: A means to an end.

Sometimes women have sex for money; they may use sex in exchange for a favor or as blackmail. Sex should not be used as a bargaining tool. This is degrading for both the man and the woman. Sex is sacred and has too many other factors with it to be used as a means to an end. When sex is used as such, people end up with are devastating consequences that may last for a lifetime.

The Root Cause

Engaging in sex or another activity to fill a void or need usually has one root cause. That root cause is not knowing or believing that God, through His son Jesus Christ, is the source for fulfillment of all your needs.

> Jesus said to them, "Very truly I tell you, it is not Moses who has given you the bread from heaven, but it is my Father who gives you the true bread from heaven. For the bread of God is the bread that comes down from heaven and gives life to the world."
>
> "Sir," they said, "always give us this bread."
>
> Then Jesus declared, "I am the bread of life. Whoever comes to me will never go hungry, and whoever believes in me will never be thirsty. But as I told you, you have seen me and still you do not believe. All those the Father gives me will come to me, and whoever comes to me I will never drive away. For I have come down from heaven not to do my will but to do the will of him who sent me. And this is the will of him who sent me, that I shall lose none of all those he has given me, but raise them up at the last day. For my Father's will is that everyone who looks

to the Son and believes in him shall have eternal life, and I will raise them up at the last day" (John 6:32-40).

Relationships with others is important. God uses others to shape us and help us grow and learn. However, nothing that we do for ourselves, or that someone else does for us, will ever match what God can do and does for us. He is the God of comfort, peace, love, grace, mercy, favor, and forgiveness. No sex, drugs, man, human love, or hugs can replace or fill us the way God fills us up.

> The Spirit alone gives eternal life. *Human effort accomplishes nothing.* And the very words I have spoken to you are spirit and life (John 6:36, emphasis added}
>
> Blessed be the God and Father of our Lord Jesus Christ, the Father of mercies and God of all comfort, who comforts us in all our affliction, so that we may be able to comfort those who are in any affliction, with the comfort with which we ourselves are comforted by God (1 Corinthians 1:3-4, ESV).
>
> "Peace I leave with you; my peace I give to you. Not as the world gives do I give to you. Let not your hearts be troubled, neither let them be afraid" (John 14:27, ESV).
>
> My beloved friends, let us continue to love each other since love comes from God. Everyone who loves is born of God and experiences a relationship with God.

> The person who refuses to love doesn't know the first thing about God, because God is love—so you can't know him if you don't love. This is how God showed his love for us: God sent his only Son into the world so we might live through him. This is the kind of love we are talking about—not that we once upon a time loved God, but that he loved us and sent his Son as a sacrifice to clear away our sins and the damage they've done to our relationship with God (1 John 4:7-10, MSG).

Whenever we try to live life on our own, we end up in failure. Blunder once or a thousand times and we hopefully come to the end of ourselves. We die.

We die to ourselves, our control issues, our sexual sin, our materialism, our drug issues, alcohols issues, perfectionism, doing good for the wrong reasons, or whatever we do to try and fill a need. It is God that we need. When we seek Him, we shall find Him. He has always been, and will always be, with us. He is our hope; He won't forsake us.

> "For I know the plans I have for you," declares the Lord, "plans for welfare and not for evil, to give you a future and a hope. Then you will call upon me and come and pray to me, and I will hear you. You will seek me and find me, when you seek me with all your heart" (Jeremiah 29:11-13, ESV).

> Keep your life free from love of money,

and be content with what you have, for he has said, "I will never leave you nor forsake you." So we can confidently say, "The Lord is my helper; I will not fear; what can man do to me?" (Hebrews 13:5-6, ESV).

We die to ourselves to live the best life in Jesus Christ.

Think on These

- It is fine to be aware of your sexuality.
- There are many reasons for sex outside of marriage, but none of them are in your best interests.
- To dig deeper into a root cause, please seek professional help.
- Sex will not satisfy a need only God can satisfy.
- Jesus is your hope, comfort, peace, love, and strength.
- What are some attributes of God? Write them down and reflect on them and how they have been present in your life.

Chapter 9

Sex Out of Order

God's will is for you to be holy, so stay away from all sexual sin. Then each of you will control his own body and live in holiness and honor— not in lustful passion like the pagans who do not know God and his ways (1 Thessalonians 4:3-5).

I originally entitled this chapter "Sexual Sin," but I changed it to not be so off-putting or to sound too judgmental. However, that is what the Bible calls it: sin. I believe the word *sin* isn't used much today because it has such a bad connotation and makes people feel bad. What other words could be used? Doing wrong, bad actions, ugly choices, evil, not doing good. Whatever words we use, they still mean the same thing: sin.

My husband and I are parents of two teen girls. It is our responsibility and duty as parents to teach our girls right and wrong. They are taught and have experienced that every choice they make has a consequence or action attached to it. They are taught about accountability for their actions and not to place blame on others for what they did.

We discipline them so they know how to establish self-discipline and self-control. They are taught about boundaries and how to establish them with themselves and others. These boundaries will help them now and in the future. They are learning how to say no when it doesn't align with their values, and what can happen if they cross boundaries, like being disrespectful to others.

We teach our daughters these things by word and action. Have you heard of the phrase "actions speak louder than words"? Many people can give lip service to their children or others about what they should do, but those same people aren't modeling what they are telling others to do. Do you understand how ineffective that is?

We both know our daughters aren't angels. But we know that the things we are modeling and telling them are catching on. When we go to their school, church, or even to their friends' houses, we are always told how good, sweet, kind, and helpful they are. We say thank you but I also say a prayer of thanks to God.

The point I'm making is: Discipline and learning to distinguish between right from wrong are things that need to continue throughout your lifetime. When you are young, it is your parents' responsibility to teach you. When you grow into adulthood, those values should be carried throughout your life. The responsibility is then on you to know right from wrong, have self-control, and to continue to have appropriate boundaries.

This discipline may hurt at the time or

be unpleasant, but in the end, it is good for you. Discipline is a loving act, done for the greater good that leads to an abundant life. Even God disciplines us, correcting us out of love.

> "Know then in your heart that, as a man disciplines his son, the Lord your God disciplines you" (Deuteronomy 8:5, ESV).

> He dies for lack of discipline, and because of his great folly he is led astray (Proverbs 5:23, ESV).

> "Those whom I love, I reprove and discipline, so be zealous and repent" (Revelation 3:19, ESV).

The Bible is the ultimate guide to what is appropriate, right, functional, and holy living. The word "guide" means a person who shows others the way, according to the *Oxford American Dictionary*. Doesn't that definition sound familiar? Who in the Bible shows us the way? Jesus does.

> Jesus told him, "I am the way, the truth, and the life. No one can come to the Father except through me" (John 14:6).

Jesus shows us the way to live by His life, His stories, and His example. God teaches us the way to live by His gift of love: the Bible. Every life circumstance we will ever encounter is dealt with in the Bible.

Contrary to what any culture may say, God wants us to live an abundant life. He loves us and has many plans and blessings for those who love and obey Him. Those plans and blessings are ours in abundance when we pray, trust, and obey God in all aspects of our daily lives.

> "Come, my children, listen to me; I will teach you the fear of the Lord. Whoever of you loves life and desires to see many good days, keep your tongue from evil and your lips from telling lies. Turn from evil and do good; seek peace and pursue it. The eyes of the Lord are on the righteous, and his ears are attentive to their cry; but the face of the Lord is against those who do evil, to blot out their name from the earth" (Psalm 34:12-16, NIV).

What is Sin?

For my purposes in this book, I use the word sin to refer to intentional sin. It is committed when an action is willfully performed on purpose while knowing it is morally questionable or wrong. Intentional sin is disobedience, done without regard for what God wants us to do: "Remember, it is sin to know what you ought to do and then not do it" (James 4:17). When we sin, we veer off the path that is the source of life. Sin brings a little death to our lives and hearts. It causes slavery, destruction, and is harmful to everyone who does it—and those closest to them.

> Do not let sin control the way you live; do not give in to sinful desires. Do not let any part of your body become an instrument of evil to serve sin. Instead, give yourselves completely to God, for you were dead, but now you have new life. So use your whole body as an instrument to

> do what is right for the glory of God. Sin is no longer your master, for you no longer live under the requirements of the law. Instead, you live under the freedom of God's grace (Romans 6:12-14).

There are countless biblical passages that refer to sexual sin, purity, and holiness. God knows how important this issue is for humans because of the powerful effects of sex—for good or bad.

> So put to death the sinful, earthly things lurking within you. Have nothing to do with sexual immorality, impurity, lust, and evil desires (Colossians 3:5).

> Finally, believers, we ask and admonish you in the Lord Jesus, that you follow the instruction that you received from us about how you ought to walk and please God (just as you are actually doing) *and that you excel even more and more [pursuing a life of purpose and living in a way that expresses gratitude to God for your salvation]* (1 Thessalonians 4:1, AMP).

> Run from sexual sin! No other sin so clearly affects the body as this one does. For sexual immorality is a sin against your own body. Don't you realize that your body is the temple of the Holy Spirit, who lives in you and was given to you by God? You do not belong to yourself, for God bought you with a high price. So you must honor God with your body (1 Corinthians 6:18-20).

Idolatry

American Idol is a reality-based music show competition that has launched the career of many contemporary singers. (Many people watch the show and enjoy it. I don't watch it because I really don't like reality shows; sometimes I want to escape reality, not re-engage it.) Some people are consumed with shows like that, making them or the participants an idol. It's no surprise they named it *American Idol*. The creators of the show knew what they were doing by using that term. There are many definitions of the word idol. *Merriam-Webster Dictionary.com* defines it as:

1. a representation or symbol of an object of worship; broadly: a false god;
2. a likeness of something;
3. obsolete, pretender, imposter;
4. a form or appearance visible but without substance;
5. an object of extreme devotion: a movie idol;
6. a false conception, untruth.

Those definitions share a common theme: falsehood and untruth. Idols are not the one true God. They are empty, unfulfilling lies that give false hope and let us down when we worship them along with God. When something takes our worship, attention, and focus away from God and Jesus, that is an idol. Sex can become an idol for some, especially if sex is used for happiness, security, to get attention, or other needs that only Jesus can fulfill. If we start to idolize sex, it can add no good to our lives.

> Therefore God gave them up in the lusts of their hearts to impurity, to the dishonoring of their bodies among themselves, because they exchanged the truth about God for a lie and worshiped and served the creature rather than the Creator, who is blessed forever! Amen (Romans 1:24-25, ESV).

Confessing Our Sins

Although God knows everything about us and what is in our hearts, He wants us to confess our sins. Continual, intentional sin and unconfessed intentional sin block blessings. Such sins can cause a lot of damage and create a life filled with unpleasant days.

> How can I know all the sins lurking in my heart? Cleanse me from these hidden faults. Keep your servant from deliberate sins! Don't let them control me. Then I will be free of guilt and innocent of great sin (Psalm 19:12-13).

Confessed intentional sin, followed by repentance (returning to a right, godly path), restores God's favor which leads to answered prayers. It enables us to fully prosper and thrive in life.

> Come and listen, all you who fear God, and I will tell you what he did for me. For I cried out to him for help, praising him as I spoke. If I had not confessed the sin in my heart, the Lord would not have listened. But God did listen! He paid attention to my prayer. Praise God,

> who did not ignore my prayer or withdraw his unfailing love from me (Psalm 66:16-20)
>
> People who conceal their sins will not prosper, but if they confess and turn from them, they will receive mercy (Proverbs 28:13).

We are to confess our sins, ask for forgiveness, repent of our wrongdoing (sin), forgive ourselves, and give thanks to Jesus. Then we should pray to the Holy Spirit, asking Him to help us remain on track, strengthening our faith and reliance on the Word, as we more fully trust and obey God. God's grace is sufficient for any situation we may face. When we do these things, we will experience some serious positive life changes. There is a whole chapter about forgiveness, repentance, and grace later in this book.

Yes, Jesus died for our sins, but that doesn't mean we are free to sin and live any way we want to. If Jesus is our Lord and Savior, He is that over our whole life. He didn't die in vain for us to do anything we want to.

> For you have been called to live in freedom, my brothers and sisters. But don't use your freedom to satisfy your sinful nature. Instead, use your freedom to serve one another in love (Galatians 5:13-14).

Fasting and Prayer

There are certain sins, strongholds, barriers, and/or decisions in our lives that require some fasting, professional help, and prayer to enable us to obtain clarity and freedom. Sexual addiction is one of those areas. Sexual addiction binds those caught up in it. Akin to habits, it enslaves people and is difficult to quit. Sexual addiction makes a person helpless and out of control. It is a compulsion that rules over those with this, or any, addiction.

The accuser, Satan, makes those bound to this sin believe the lies that he tells them. He makes them believe that they are helpless, that this is their lot and that they can't be delivered from it. But guess what? Satan is a liar! He is the great deceiver, but we have power over him and his lies. Sexual addiction is a sin that has an external pull. A person can be delivered from it through prayer and fasting. *The Disciple's Fast*[1]-deals with this type of bondage.

> You are wrestling for control of your life when you enter The Disciple's Fast. By controlling what you eat, you determine that you will control your life for God's purpose. When you make a vow and reinforce it with The Disciple's Fast, you move into the strength of decision making. You give up necessary or enjoyable food as a demonstration of the commitment of your will. When you make a choice to fast, you strengthen yourself to stand against a force that has enslaved your spiritual appetite. In The Disciple's Fast you control your physical appetite to strengthen your spiritual appetite[1]

I recommend reading tist book to get more information and clarity concerning *The Disciple's Fast* and other fasts which will help lead you to a spiritual breakthrough.

As I mentioned at the beginning of this section, in additional to fasting I recommend professional help along with having a group of loving, honest friends to help you find deliverance from sexual or any other type of addiction. It is hard to do it alone.

The Power of the Holy Spirit

We are to live by the power of the Holy Spirit! We are made to crave God and the power of the Holy Spirit. The Holy Spirit assists us so we can keep sin out of our lives. When we continue to be in God's Word, receive the infilling of the Holy Spirit and living by that same Spirit, it is a high like no other. The Spirit of God brings life and peace.

> Now the mind of the flesh is death [both now and forever—because it pursues sin]; but the mind of the Spirit is life and peace [the spiritual well-being that comes from walking with God—both now and forever] (Romans 8:6, AMP).

I love to worship God in song. I feel the Spirits' presence during powerful, communal church worship. My eyes tear and my heart wells with joy. Peace and emotions I can't explain bombard my soul. That's being high on the Holy Spirit. Have you ever felt that? You can also experience this high daily by reading God's Word daily. Praise and worship Him. Meditate on the Scriptures and bask in His love and goodness. I continually experience this kind of high, exhilaration that only comes from God.

God's Instructions

God doesn't give us only "what not to do's."

He gives us instructions on how to live godly, functional, righteous lives. The blessings and promises we receive when we live those lives are explained as well. The Bible equips believers to do what God has purposed for them.

> All Scripture is God-breathed and is useful for teaching, rebuking, correcting and training in righteousness, so that the servant of God may be thoroughly equipped for every good work (2 Timothy 3:16, NIV).

Jesus' *Sermon on the Mount and the Beatitudes were* great descriptions of the blessings we receive when we live godly, Christ-like lives. This can be called a "Cliff Notes" version:

> Now when Jesus saw the crowds, He went up on a mountainside and sat down. His disciples came to Him, and He began to teach them. He said: "Blessed are the poor in spirit, for theirs is the kingdom of heaven. Blessed are those who mourn, for they will be comforted. Blessed are the meek, for they will inherit the earth. Blessed are those who hunger and thirst for righteousness, for they will be filled. Blessed are the merciful, for they will be shown mercy. Blessed are the pure in heart, for they will see God. Blessed are the peacemakers, for they will be called children of God. Blessed are those who are persecuted because of righteousness, for theirs is the kingdom of heaven. Blessed are you when people insult you,

persecute you and falsely say all kinds of evil against you because of me. Rejoice and be glad, because great is your reward in heaven, for in the same way they persecuted the prophets who were before you" (Matthew 5:1-12, NIV).

Aren't those blessings powerful? My heart wells up with gladness, hope, and joy when I think of all the blessings God promised and has already given to me. Most of these blessings are activated by prayer and living like Jesus Christ by the power of the Holy Spirit.

What is a Blessing?

There are different definitions of blessings in the Bible according to how they are used, but one thing is consistent: They are all positive. "Two distinct ideas are present. First, a blessing was a public declaration of a favored status with God. Second, the blessing endowed power for prosperity and success."[2]

Bless is from the Hebrew word *barak*, which means *to kneel and show respect*. Another definition of blessings is: a sign of God's favor that results in the Holy Spirit (spiritual blessings), affluence, victory, joy and prosperity. All this is available when we accept that we can't succeed in life alone without God. Believe in Jesus as your Lord and Savior, pray, trust and obey. Thank You, Lord, for blessing us!

Getting Back on Track

Don't get me wrong, it is not always easy to do what is right and follow God's path and today's cultural environment depicts sex *everywhere*. Our carnal mind thinking it knows what is best for us.

When we listen to the advice of our flesh or follow its urgings, we find ourselves derailed, off track, hurting, alone, and not where God intended for us to be. I've gotten off track numerous times.

Thanks be to God for our Savior Jesus whose death on the cross sustains us when we veer off course due to our mistakes, which are often willful. Yes, we will experience the consequences of bad choices; sometimes they are lifelong, painful, and life-altering. However, Jesus is always there, helping us get back on track through His unfailing love and faithfulness. I am not trying to shame or heap guilt on you. We all have sin resumes. God bestows no shame, guilt, or condemnation when we veer off track. He wants us to stay on the path that leads to abundant life, and will get us back on track if we so choose.

> There is therefore now no condemnation to them which are in Christ Jesus, who walk not after the flesh, but after the Spirit. For the law of the Spirit of life in Christ Jesus hath made me free from the law of sin and death (Romans 8:1-2, KJV).

We are called to help other Christians get over their sin, helping them not to stumble again while we lift one another up in prayer and through encouragement. God has called me to write this book to fortify and strengthen women with the truth of His love so they will know His design for sex, grace, forgiveness, and mercy. This armor of God helps us to stand guard, stay strong in our faith, be brave, and pursue the life of peace, blessings, and happiness He intended for all of us—including you.

Things to Think On

- You are in control of your actions.
- Set boundaries in your life. Be able to say no and yes with confidence.
- *Sin* causes you to veer of the path of life God has for you.
- *Intentional sin* is done on purpose, with no regrets; a willful disobedience.
- Jesus died for your sins; they are wiped clean! Believe it and receive it.
- Confess your sins, ask for forgiveness, repent, and turn your life around; start anew.
- There is no shame, condemnation, or guilt in Jesus.
- God loves you with an everlasting love.

Chapter 10

The Aftershock of Sex

Trust God from the bottom of your heart; don't try to figure out everything on your own. Listen for God's voice in everything you do, everywhere you go; he's the one who will keep you on track (Proverbs 3:5-6, MSG).

As stated previously and repeatedly, all actions have consequences. The choices you make—good or bad—trigger chain reactions. These reverberate throughout the world and affect everyone. Glory to Jesus for freeing us from our sins! However, we still must live with the consequences of our actions. One of the most obvious results of sex is pregnancy. Making babies, being fruitful, and multiplying or procreation are the main functions God designed sex to fulfill. In addition to the visible results, there are unseen consequences of sex. The ramifications are emotional, biblical, and physical. These effects may last for a lifetime.

Emotional Consequences: Pain From Bond Breaks

The brain gets used to the influx of dopamine, oxytocin, and vasopressin that comes from intimate, sexual, and close contact with another person. These bonds get stronger with each sexual act. Addiction to each other occurs. When the relationship ends and sexual contact stops, the effects are like a drug withdrawal. There are physical withdrawal symptoms that can be experienced, things llike Depression, insomnia, loss of appetite, anxiety, and invasive thoughts.[1] These symptoms won't last forever, but they will be around for about six months or more. The time varies depending upon a person's coping skills.

When a person keeps hooking up and breaking up, it will be harder to bond and have a lasting relationship with another person. The brain and heart don't like the pain from the bond breaking and it will try to be protective against the pain, which eventually causes a hardened heart and/or a pattern of serial relationships. A serious relationship can develop after that, but it will take prayer, deliverance, some professional help, intention, and awareness of behaviors to succeed.

Worldly Consequences: Names Can Hurt

The culture advises people to *have sex with whomever you please. YOLO, get it girl!* Yet if a girl has sex with multiple partners, she is called fast, a slut, thot, or whatever new label there is. This can be very confusing and hurtful for some young women, especially teens, because they are still maturing and trying to find out who they are. I discussed identity in a previous chapter, but I will repeat what I wrote again: Our identity as women is not and should not be based on sex, sexuality, or sexual preference. It may be a part of us, but it doesn't make us who we are. God makes us who we are through His son Jesus—our identity is found in Christ.

Remember, just because the culture approves it doesn't make it right. Don't do things simply because others are doing them! You are strong, bright, valuable, and smart. Take the time to think before acting. Be armed with knowledge so you can make better life decisions.

> For everything in the world—the lust of the flesh, the lust of the eyes, and the pride of life—comes not from the Father but from the world. The world and its desires pass away, but whoever does the will of God lives forever (1John 2:16-17, NIV).

Biblical Consequences

I know I have talked about this before, but it is so important. Sex outside of or apart from God's design is a sin against God and our bodies—for both Christians *and* non-Christians. As a Christian, we have the Holy Spirit dwelling within us. When sexual sin occurs, it defiles the temple (our body) of the Holy Spirit. When we have sex with someone, God is part of that union. He becomes an observer of the sin. Picture Jesus standing right beside you all the time. Wou;dn't that make you think differently about sex?

> God honored the Master's body by raising it from the grave. He'll treat yours with the same resurrection power.

> Until that time, remember that your bodies are created with the same dignity as the Master's body. You wouldn't take the Master's body off to a whorehouse, would you? I should hope not (1 Corinthians 6:14-15, MSG).

Sexual sin grieves the Holy Spirit (makes him sad) and will result in conviction: the little tug in your heart that lets you know you dishonored God. Listen to it, ask for forgiveness, and be actively aware of the triggers of sexual sin to avoid falling into it again. It's important to know that God forgives and takes away the sin, but there are still consequences involved with the decision to have sex. I will talk more about God's grace and forgiveness in the next chapter.

> There's more to sex than mere skin on skin. Sex is as much spiritual mystery as physical fact. As written in Scripture, "The two become one." Since we want to become spiritually one with the Master, we must not pursue the kind of sex that avoids commitment and intimacy, leaving us more lonely than ever— the kind of sex that can never "become one." There is a sense in which sexual sins are different from all others. In sexual sin we violate the sacredness of our own bodies, these bodies that were made for God-given and God-modeled love, for "becoming one" with another. Or didn't you realize that your body is a sacred place, the place of the Holy Spirit?

Don't you see that you can't live however you please, squandering what God paid such a high price for? The physical part of you is not some piece of property belonging to the spiritual part of you. God owns the whole works. So let people see God in and through your body (1 Corinthians 6:16-20, MSG)

I love *The Message Bible's* version of 1 Corinthians 6:16-20 quoted above. We bond with whomever we have sex with. Spiritually and physically, a part of the women is always with the man and vice versa. This applies to *everyone* because chemical bonds are made through the sexual act. Don't let Jesus' death for our sins be in vain. God wants us to be <u>one flesh</u> with our husbands only. The marriage union is an important demonstration of God's special and intimate union with us, His people.

Physical Consequences: Pregnancy

Let's talk about the birds and bees ... that was an old code for the baby-making "sex talk." I covered some of this information in Chapter 2 during our discussion on menstruation. I'll repeat some of it now for a purpose. A baby can be made when a man and woman have sexual intercourse. Conception occurs when the sperm from the man fertilizes the woman's egg. Lots of things happens with cell division and other awesome miracles from that point on. Nine to ten months later, a baby is born. This is the number one biological reason for having sexual intercourse. Important news: Pregnancy can still take place even if birth control and condoms are used!

Sexually Transmitted Diseases or Infections – STD/STI

STDs or STIs are diseases and infections that are passed by intimate and sexual contact with another person. Over the years, rates of infections have been steadily rising and are at record highs. Young people ages 15-24 and pregnant women are more affected by STDs. Studies find young women are more susceptible to contracting chlamydia, HIV, and HPV because of cervical ectopy.[2] Cervical ectopy is a type of columnar cell found during life stages.[2] Adolescence and pregnancy are some life stages

Here is a list of some of the most common STD's /STI's found at CDC.gov:

- Bacterial Vaginosis
- Chlamydia
- Gonorrhea
- Genital Herpes
- HIV/AIDS
- Human Papilloma Virus (HPV)
- Pelvic Inflammatory Disease (PID)
- Syphilis
- Hepatitis
- Trichomoniasis
- Mycoplasma genitalium

In my job as a medical laboratory professional, I regular performed urinalysis tests. At times while looking under the microscope to check urine and vaginal swabs, Trichomoniasis critters were viewed. They look like little bugs with cilia (tiny hairs that move) and a tail whipping around to help them move. These are living things that want to make humans their home. (If nothing else stops you from having sex, this should.) Here are some shocking statistics of three reportable STIs in the U.S.

1. Chlamydia[4] – 1,649,716 cases in 2022 (most recent report).[3] This is a -6.2% percent change since 2018 according to the CDC's Sexually Transmitted Infection surveillance in 2022. Early infection of chlamydia in women is asymptomatic. In other words, it means there are no symptoms. Diagnosis is found through testing. If left untreated, it can cause pelvic inflammatory disease (PID). PID causes inflammation and damage to fallopian tubes which can cause infertility and/or ectopic pregnancy.

2. Gonorrhea[5] – 648,056 cases[3]. This represents an 11 % increase since 2018. Early infection of gonorrhea is also asymptomatic in women. What's more, gonorrhea can cause PID if left untreated.

3. Syphilis (all phases)[6] – 203,500 cases[2]. This number represents a 78.9 percent increase since 2018. Syphilis infection has three phases. Each phase has different symptoms. If not treated, syphilis can be dormant in the body for a few years then start

affecting the heart, brain, eyes, and internal organs, eventually causing death.

Here is some important information to remember about sexually transmitted infections and diseases:

- Some of the infections are caused by bacteria and may be cured with antibiotics.
- Some of these are viruses and can't be cured. There are medications that can help with symptoms and outbreaks of viruses. HIV and Herpes are examples of lifelong diseases.
- You can't always tell if someone has an STD by looking at them (or their body parts).
- Getting tested for STD/STIs is the only way to know if someone is infected.
- Some diseases can cause infertility, leaving a woman unable to get pregnant and/or can cause miscarriage.
- If infected during pregnancy, STDs can cause premature delivery, premature rupture of the membranes, low birth weight, conjunctivitis, and stillbirth.
- Condoms lower the risk for infection, but they are not 100% effective.
- No method of protection is 100% effective. The only method that truly

- protects any one from an STD is abstinence (no sex).
- Although there is new medicine that may help reduce the risk of HIV/AIDS transmission rates, it is not 100% effective. And it still doesn't stop the bonding and other problems that sex can cause.
- Visit the Center for Disease Control website—CDC.gov— for in-depth info on all STDs and STIs.

If you had sex, protected or unprotected, please get tested for STDs/STIs. It can save your life and those of your future children. Local health departments, hospitals, doctors, and some pregnancy resource centers offer no- or low-cost testing.

Sex and Pornographic Addictions

Addiction is a treatable, chronic medical disease involving complex interactions among brain circuits, genetics, the environment, and an individual's life experiences as defined by the American Society of Addiction Medicine.[7]

Sexual addiction is real and prevalent in the culture today; it affects 3%-6% of adults.[8] Sex addiction or hypersexual disorder is characterized by a compulsive need for instant gratification of sexual urges.[9] This malady affects Christians and non-Christians alike. Sex addiction in women is a growing concern in the United States. Dopamine is the primary suspect responsible for addiction. Sexual addiction includes behaviors such as extramarital affairs, excessive use of pornography, online sex, extreme sexting, compulsive masturbation, exhibitionism, voyeurism, and prostitution.[8] With the advent of internet pornography and online dating sites, sexual addiction has of course increased.

Although sex is a natural behavior, it is considered an addiction or compulsion when the behavior supersedes reason, logic, will-power, and self-control. Desire elicits an explosive surge release of dopamine and the glorious feeling of pleasure results. Some people become addicted to the feeling of gratification. Remember, dopamine urges us to want something that we may not particularly like or that is not in our best interests.

If you or someone you love is showing signs of addiction, please go get help. Addiction is a disease that should not be taken lightly.

Think On These

- Pregnancy and STDs are physical consequences of sex.
- Emotional consequences like depression, regret, and guilt may be experienced from sexual sin/sex before marriage.
- Being known for a one's sexual activity is a worldly trait and has no place in God's Kingdom.
- Sinning against our body, God, and the Holy Spirit result in consequences of sexual sin clearly explained in the Bible.

Chapter 11

God's Design for Sex

Drink water from your own well— share your love only with your wife. Why spill the water of your springs in the streets, having sex with just anyone? You should reserve it for yourselves. Never share it with strangers (Proverbs 5:15-17).

     God designed sex to be much more than a means to personal fulfillment. Sex is sacred. It is for a husband and wife to procreate (be fruitful and multiply) and for them to bond and to become one in marital harmony (where two become one flesh). It involves emotional, spiritual, and physical components all working together. It is more than just having sex; it is making love.

     I love the verse I included at the beginning of this chapter. *Never share it (sex) with strangers.* Husbands know, and will know, more about their wives than any man she might have dated. There is an intimacy that is only shared between a husband and wife once they have made a marriage covenant.

That is why a man leaves his father and mother and is united to his wife, and they become one flesh (Genesis 2:24, NIV).

Let marriage be held in honor among all, and let the marriage bed be undefiled, for God will judge the sexually immoral and adulterous (Hebrews 13:4, ESV)

Marriage Matters

Marriage is not to be taken lightly because it is a covenant, and God is a covenant-making and covenant-keeping God. "A covenant is a serious binding agreement between two parties—one that carries with it not only certain blessings but also responsibilities. A covenant carries with it a sense of connectedness of two becoming one." This definition is from Kay Arthur's *Covenant: God's Enduring Promises* Bible study workbook (one of the most life-changing Bible studies I was ever a part of). Covenants involve both sacrifice and celebration.

The covenant or binding agreement is between three parties: the man, the woman, and God. The Lord is the witness in the marriage covenant. Each party in this agreement has certain responsibilities to uphold. For example, consider the wedding vows: for richer or poorer, in sickness and health, etc. Those are some of the responsibilities the husband and wife agree to uphold. Once made, God's blessing and covering are upon this covenant.

The marriage covenant is similar to the New Covenant made with its Peacemaker, Jesus. Jesus is God's covenant with us. Jesus established the blood covenant that covers our sins and forgives us, and represents the entrance to heaven for each of us.

> This is the covenant I will establish with the people of Israel after that time, declares the Lord. I will put my laws in their mind and write them on their hearts. I will be their God, and they will be my people. No longer will they teach their neighbor, or say to one another, 'Know the Lord,' because they will all know me, from the least of them to the greatest. For I will forgive their wickedness and will remember their sins no more (Hebrews 8:10-12, NIV).

As wives, we can be emotionally, spiritually, mentally, and physically naked and comfortable in front of our husbands, knowing they love us inside and out. Sex is an act of worship that a husband and wife perform together to fulfill God's command. The pleasure of sex is a result (a bonus).

A healthy marriage represents the relationship between Jesus and the Church (His followers). God wants husbands to love their wives with the same great love He has for the church. Wives are to respect their husbands as the Church respects Jesus' authority. What a powerful message that proclaims to the world

> Husbands, go all out in your love for your wives, exactly as Christ did for the church—a love marked by giving, not getting. Christ's love makes the church whole. His words evoke her beauty. Everything he does and says is designed to bring the best out of her, dressing her in dazzling white silk, radiant with

> holiness. And that is how husbands ought to love their wives. They're really doing themselves a favor—since they're already "one" in marriage.
>
> No one abuses his own body, does he? No, he feeds and pampers it. That's how Christ treats us, the church, since we are part of his body. And this is why a man leaves father and mother and cherishes his wife. No longer two, they become "one flesh." This is a huge mystery, and I don't pretend to understand it all. What is clearest to me is the way Christ treats the church. And this provides a good picture of how each husband is to treat his wife, loving himself in loving her, and how each wife is to honor her husband (Ephesians 5:22-33, MSG).

There is freedom in the choice to wait for marriage to have sex. When we choose to wait to have sex with our husbands, we are obeying God and we are on the right path regarding the role of sex as God intended.

Our lives should be pleasing to God and the Bible tells us how to go about living in such a way. The Bible is God's manual for right living. He wants us to be sanctified and righteous and He gives us the words and actions for how to do that in His good book. Sanctification takes time and action; it occurs by being intentional and through obeying the Holy Spirit.

> It is God's will that you should be sanctified: that you should avoid sexual

immorality; that each of you should learn to control your own body in a way that is holy and honorable, not in passionate lust like the pagans, who do not know God (1 Thessalonians 4:3-5, NIV).

God has grace and forgives those who are truly sorry for indulging in sex out of His prescribed order. This sorrow is not a worldly sorrow that points out how bad or evil we are, but a godly sorrow because of how much we have offended God and damaged ourselves. This truth about sex is given to stop the lies the world and the devil spread about sex. Turn away from sex, honor God and your body, and choose to wait for your husband (or wife for any man reading this).

If you are not a Christian, I pray this book will enlighten you with the truth and open your heart to God's love. It is wise to stop having sex and wait for your spouse. Sex is not meant to be had with many partners because it will make you oblivious to the consequences and can cause you to miss out on the fulfillment of sex with your future spouse.

Think On These

- God's design for sex is with a husband and wife.
- Marriage is a covenant between God, a husband, and wife—a binding agreement. Each party agrees to do their part to uphold the agreement.
- A husband and wife share the most intimate bond there is.

Chapter 12

The Truth About God's Grace and Forgiveness

I do not treat the grace of God as meaningless. For if keeping the law could make us right with God, then there was no need for Christ to die (Galatians 2:21).

While working at the Pregnancy Resource Center, I met some Christian young ladies (even some preachers' daughters) who were sexually active, had multiple pregnancies, and even abortions. They had little knowledge about God's design for sex. They were confused concerning how to live a righteous life. One woman told me, "God forgives me, so I'll do it any way" when contemplating abortion. When she told me that, my heart stopped. Deception concerning sin, forgiveness, and God's grace had clouded her judgement.

I explained those concepts to her, but the emotions crowding her mind from the crisis and trauma she was experiencing overtook wisdom. Our contact became less frequent and eventually she stopped communicating altogether. I pray God gave her the full knowledge of His love, grace, and forgiveness so she could adjust her lifestyle and make better decisions.

Full understanding of grace and forgiveness is lacking in many Christian circles. This ignorance brings spiritual death to numerous lives. So let's spend some time discussing grace and forgiveness, because they are crucial to a healthy and righteous relationship between God and His people. It is part of living an abundant life.

> Get rid of all bitterness, rage, anger, harsh words, and slander, as well as all types of evil behavior. Instead, be kind to each other, tenderhearted, forgiving one another, just as God through Christ has forgiven you (Ephesians 4:31-32).

As I talk about God's grace and truth, remember God's love for you. God, who is your Father in heaven, is like any other parent who loves their children. He wants what is best for you and has a guidebook, the Bible, to help you live your best life. God's design for sex should be experienced between a husband and wife. Therefore, sex is worth waiting for and a means of great pleasure if limited to marriage.

If you have had sex out of order before you were married, you are right in thinking it is not the end of the world. From personal experience, I know that for a fact. My world didn't end. However, you are naïve if you think there are not consequences because there are. I suffered consequences. I wish I could turn back time and choose differently. Although I was not able to do that, I did have the ability to repent and ask God to forgive me. The good news is God extends His grace and He forgives, but the consequences remain as does God's grace and forgiveness.

God's Grace

Grace is God's favor, goodwill, mercy, and kindness. In Greek, the word is *xaris*; the transliteration is *charis*[1] which means grace and kindness.[1] I like the word *grace*. When I think of grace, a picture of a ballerina comes to mind. The word reminds me of things of beauty because grace is a thing of beauty. Thank You, Lord! A biblical lexicon provides meanings and uses of biblical words in their original language. The *Helps Word Studies Biblical Lexicon* describes grace as,

> Cognate: 5485 *xáris* (another feminine noun from *xar-*, "*favor, disposed to, inclined, favor*able towards, *leaning towards* to share benefit») – properly, *grace*. 5485 (*xáris*) is preeminently used of the Lord's *favor* – freely *extended to give Himself* away to people (because He is «always leaning toward them»).[2]

What comes to mind with that description of God leaning toward the world to give Himself to us? For me, that is an accurate and fantastic description of grace. We are favored by God. God's grace is a gift bestowed through our Lord Jesus Christ. What is so awesome about grace is that we don't deserve it. We are born with the stain of sin on us, but God is willing to overlook that and restore us to a right relationship with Him—by and through His grace.

> For everyone has sinned; we all fall short of God's glorious standard (Romans 3:23).

That verse from Romans contains a sobering truth, but because of God's love for us, He has given us a chance to overcome our sing and be intimate with Him through His son Jesus. Instead of receiving the death we deserve, we are given a choice and a chance for life—His divine, eternal life. That's grace.

> Yet God, in his grace, freely makes us right in his sight. He did this through Christ Jesus when he freed us from the penalty for our sins. For God presented Jesus as the sacrifice for sin. People are made right with God when they believe that Jesus sacrificed his life, shedding his blood (Romans 3:24-25a).

I want to stress the part of that passage that states "when they believe that Jesus sacrificed his life." In order to appropriate this grace, we must believe and have a firm commitment to Jesus as our Savior or the grace doesn't need to be given. God gives us a choice. Grace is the gift of salvation for all people!

> For the grace of God has appeared, bringing salvation for all people, training us to renounce ungodliness and worldly passions, and to live self-controlled,

> upright, and godly lives in the present age, waiting for our blessed hope, the appearing of the glory of our great God and Savior Jesus Christ, who gave himself for us to redeem us from all lawlessness and to purify for himself a people for his own possession who are zealous for good works (Titus 2:11-14, ESV).

> Sin is no longer your master, for you no longer live under the requirements of the law. Instead, you live under the freedom of God's grace (Romans 6:14, NIV).

There is much more to grace than God's favor and goodwill. Grace strengthens us. Grace assists in to avoid sin and maintains us through faith. Grace influences our hearts to live a life pleasing to God. It frees us from sin as we walk in obedience and is a source for our blessings. God's grace points us towards Jesus and then helps us walk the path.

Grace is a power that only comes through faith in Jesus Christ. Grace is given to those who are humble and who put their trust in Jesus. Be willing to receive God's grace and be thankful for the grace He gives. Grace is a supernatural power that can keep us away from sexual sin. Acknowledge and then abide in the power of grace in your life.

> But by the grace of God I am what I am, and his grace toward me was not in vain. On the contrary, I worked harder than any of them, though it was not I, but the grace of God that is with me (1 Corinthians 15:10, ESV).

Don't be a slave to sexual sin. Speak of the power of grace in your life. Meditate, write down, and speak aloud these Bible verses pertaining to grace. Pray, trust in, and obey Jesus. Believe you are worthy to be loved and live by the Holy Spirit. His grace gives us the power to turn from sexual sin.

> Grace and peace to you many times over as you deepen in your experience with God and Jesus, our Master. Everything that goes into a life of pleasing God has been miraculously given to us by getting to know, personally and intimately, the One who invited us to God. The best invitation we ever received (2 Peter 1:2-4, MSG).

> For we do not have a high priest who is unable to sympathize with our weaknesses, but one who in every respect has been tempted as we are, yet without sin. Let us then with confidence draw near to the throne of grace, that we may receive mercy and find grace to help in time of need (Hebrews 4:15-16, ESV).

I remind you of what I wrote earlier about the word grace creating a picture in my mind of a ballerina. Grace is both beauty and power, elegance and purpose, just like a ballerina. Ballet dancers are strong yet graceful, elegant but flowing with purpose. They are a beauty to behold and so is grace operating in our lives.

Forgiveness

Do you have credit card bills? Pay rent or

have a mortgage? Do you owe anyone money? If you answered yes to any of these questions, what if you didn't have to pay back any of the money you owed? What if your account was zeroed out and wiped clean? Maybe an unknown donor paid it, or the company gave you a break. Any way it happened, it's all good! That's cause for a happy dance.

That is what forgiveness is like. Our debts and loans, or in this case our sins, are pardoned or wiped clean. God sent Jesus Christ to reconcile us to Himself. Jesus received the penalty of death for our sin debt. Jesus paid for all our sins, wrongdoing, bad thoughts, sexual sins, gossiping, hatred, lying. Jesus sacrificed Himself for us. He is the only true superhero, a real Superman or Marvel Avenger.

> For this is my blood of the covenant, which is poured out for many for the forgiveness of sins (Matthew 26:28, ESV).
>
> For God so loved the world, that he gave his only begotten Son, that whosoever believeth in him should not perish, but have everlasting life. For God sent not his Son into the world to condemn the world; but that the world through him might be saved. He that believeth on him is not condemned: but he that believeth not is condemned already, because he hath not believed in the name of the only begotten Son of God (John 3:16-18, KJV).

How awesome is that? It doesn't matter how many times I read or hear those verses. I am always grateful, amazed, in awe, and filled with love at how much God loves me and the world! Thank You, Lord, for loving us so much!

Confessing

Although Jesus died for our sins and wiped the slate clean, we still need to confess those intentional sins, ask forgiveness, repent, and move forward doing the right thing. Jesus didn't die for us to keep on sinning and do whatever we want to do.

> If we confess our sins, he is faithful and just and will forgive us our sins and purify us from all unrighteousness (1 John 1:9, NIV).

> People who conceal their sins will not prosper, but if they confess and turn from them, they will receive mercy (Proverbs 28:13).

> What shall we say, then? Shall we go on sinning so that grace may increase? By no means! We are those who have died to sin; how can we live in it any longer? (Romans 6:1-2, NIV).

If Jesus Christ is your Lord and Savior, you are free from it all! No stain, no chains, no guilt, no shame. Believe it in your heart of hearts and live a life pleasing God. Death to all that you are trying to be, or think you need to be, when it comes to sexual sin.

> So now there is no condemnation for those who belong to Christ Jesus (Romans 8:1).

> I have been crucified with Christ [that is, in Him I have shared His crucifixion]; it

> is no longer I who live, but Christ lives in me. The life I now live in the body I live by faith [by adhering to, relying on, and completely trusting] in the Son of God, who loved me and gave Himself up for me (Galatians 2:20, AMP)

When Jesus is your Savior, the Spirit of God lives in you. When you live according to the Spirit, your mind is set on what He desires. It is your love for God that motivates you to do what is pleasing to Him instead of that which is displeases Him. Romans 8:1-15 explains this well; read it, write it, memorize it!

Repentance

After asking for forgiveness, repentance follows. To repent means to feel such sorrow for one's sins or faults as to be disposed to change one's life for the better, according to the *Oxford American Dictionary*. In other words, we are to stop doing that which is displeasing to God and start doing the things that please Him and make our life better. It is having a godly sorrow, not a worldly, prideful sorrow. Worldly sorrows care about what others think of us; the wrong we did makes us look bad to others. Godly sorrow is humbling.

> For the kind of sorrow God wants us to experience leads us away from sin and results in salvation. There's no regret for that kind of sorrow. But worldly sorrow, which lacks repentance, results in spiritual death (2 Corinthians 7:10).

> God overlooked people's ignorance about these things in earlier times, but

now he commands everyone everywhere to repent of their sins and turn to him (Acts 17:30).

> Those whom I [dearly and tenderly] love, I rebuke and discipline [showing them their faults and instructing them]; so be enthusiastic and repent [change your inner self—your old way of thinking, your sinful behavior—seek God's will] (Revelation 3:19, AMP).

This is not the same as shame or guilt. Before Jesus died for our sins, we were found guilty and condemned under the law of God. When Adam and Eve sinned, we were separated from God and death was the penalty. We were guilty because of our sins, but Jesus came and died on the cross to erase the guilt and shame. We are now no longer found guilty because He paid our debts.

> Therefore, there is now no condemnation for those who are in Christ Jesus, because through Christ Jesus the law of the Spirit who gives life has set you free from the law of sin and death. For what the law was powerless to do because it was weakened by the flesh, God did by sending his own Son in the likeness of sinful flesh to be a sin offering. And so he condemned sin in the flesh, in order that the righteous requirement of the law might be fully met in us, who do not live according to the flesh but according to the Spirit (Romans 8:1-4, NIV).

If you have some sexual sin in your life and are heartily sorry for disobeying God, confess your sins, ask for forgiveness, stop committing the sexual sin (repent), and start obeying the Lord. I promise that you will be blessed; what's more important, God promises the same thing. It may be hard at first but endure. Trust in the Lord and His grace will give you will power over sin.

Faith in Jesus gives you authority and power over fear, sins, worry, anxiety, and other negative things. You are given the spirit of power, love, a sound mind and self – control (see 2 Timothy 1:7) Let no sin rule over you.

> Direct my footsteps according to your word; let no sin rule over me (Psalm 119:133, NIV).

It's hard to live right for God if you are not in fellowship with other believers. Therefore, stay in close relationships with other believers. Have relationships with others who extend grace and love; you help each other not to stumble.

Mercy

Being merciful is another quality of God. It is an aspect of justice that is grouped with grace and forgiveness. It is a characteristic similar to grace and forgiveness which Christians should also model. Mercy is an implied fruit of the Spirit. *Oxford American Dictionary* defines mercy as "refraining from inflicting punishment or pain from an offender or enemy etc. who is in one's power."

Suppose you were notified of your credit card being used by an unknown person. The bank stopped the charges and the offender was in custody at the police station. The bank wants to press charges but you show mercy and tell them to release him as you don't want to punish him for his wrongdoing. That is similar to what God does. He shows us mercy from the countless offenses we have committed against Him and others. He doesn't give us the punishment we deserve—namely death. Mercy is shown through Jesus' sacrifice on the cross.

> Here is a trustworthy saying that deserves full acceptance: Christ Jesus came into the world to save sinners—of whom I am the worst. But for that very reason I was shown mercy so that in me, the worst of sinners, Christ Jesus might display his immense patience as an example for those who would believe in him and receive eternal life (1 Timothy 1:15-16, NIV).
>
> But when the kindness and love of God our Savior appeared, he saved us, not because of righteous things we had done, but because of his mercy. He saved us through the washing of rebirth and renewal by the Holy Spirit, whom he poured out on us generously through Jesus Christ our Savior, so that, having been justified by his grace, we might become heirs having the hope of eternal life (Titus 3:4-7, NIV).
>
> "Blessed are the merciful, for they shall receive mercy" (Matthew 5:7, NASB).

Thank you Lord, for giving us mercy, grace, forgiveness and Your ultimate unfailing love.

I'm going to end this chapter with two of my favorite verses (I have a lot of favorites as you can tell). This passage is powerful and shows clearly what Jesus did for us and what He still does. This is written down in my prayer journal and I frequently speak it outloud:

> To him who is able to keep you from stumbling and to present you before his glorious presence without fault and with great joy—to the only God our Savior be glory, majesty, power and authority, through Jesus Christ our Lord, before all ages, now and forevermore! Amen (Jude 24-25, NIV).

Here is a sample prayer of forgiveness you can use as a guide when you pray to the Lord:

Dear Lord,

I praise and worship Your holy name. You're so good. I ask You to forgive me of my sins (insert your specific sin or sins here). Thank You for loving me so much that You sent Your son to be punished and die in my place for the sins I have committed. Thank You for forgiving me. I'm sorry from the bottom of my heart, and I want to do the right thing. Create a clean heart in me and let no sin rule over me. Thank You for the power of grace. I trust You, Jesus. Thank You for loving me! I love You! To God be the glory.

In Jesus' name I pray, amen.

Think On These

- God's grace is a gift that is freely given.
- Grace comes through faith in Jesus. Have you accepted God's gift of grace?
- Forgiveness is a pardon of the wrong that was done.
- Confess all intentional and unknowing sins daily.
- Repentance is being truly sorry for the wrong you have done and letting God know we truly want to change our way of living.
- Mercy is not giving us the punishment we deserve.
- When you have sex out of order, you will experience consequences.
- Guilt and shame are gone through Jesus' sacrifice.
- God wants to help you, not harm you.
- God loves you … and so do I!

Chapter 13

More Than Boobs and Booty

For we are God's masterpiece. He has created us anew in Christ Jesus, so we can do the good things he planned for us long ago (Ephesians 2:10).

Let's say you are scrolling through Instagram, Snapchat, Twitter or Facebook and you see gorgeous women with perfect hair, bodies, teeth, and clothes. You double tap, click the heart or thumbs up, and keep scrolling, wishing you could get that haircut, buy that sleek outfit, or sculpt that cute booty. Sadly, you are slowly chipping away at the beauty of your own uniqueness.

Social media can be a tremendous tool for work, entertainment, causes, or other activities, and the worst vehicle for someone with anxiety, low self-worth, or imposter's syndrome. False, photo-shopped, and filtered images on social media deceive viewers.

You start comparing yourself to others and anxiety increases. There is good news, however, something that may help lower anxiety and raise your self-worth: *There is no one who can compare to you! You are precious in God's eyes.*

There is a lie commonly circulated that a woman's worth is dependent upon her body, looks, and sex. That is far from the truth—those things don't determine a woman's value. Your worth is defined by God's view and acceptance of you. God loves you so much that He sent His Son to die for you. I know, I am repeating this, but it's true, important, and life-changing. Despite your flaws and imperfections, God sees you as worth dying for. You are precious in His sight. Believe it!

> "Are not five sparrows sold for two pennies? Yet not one of them is forgotten by God. Indeed, the very hairs of your head are all numbered. Don't be afraid; you are worth more than many sparrows" (Luke 12:6-7, NIV).

> "Look at the birds of the air: they neither sow nor reap nor gather into barns, and yet your heavenly Father feeds them. Are you not of more value than they?" (Matthew 6:26, ESV).

God created women as creatures of beauty. I consider the word *beauty* to be feminine. Pictures and words that come to my mind when thinking of beauty are flowers, serenity, symmetry, and flow. What comes to your mind when defining beauty?

God made you as His beautiful poem, a work of art. You are unique and one of a kind. You are special and have a special place in this world. Please don't let the culture, men, other women or anybody's stereotypical definition override what God says about you as a woman.

> For you created my inmost being; you knit me together in my mother's womb. I praise you because I am fearfully and wonderfully made; your works are wonderful, I know that full well. My frame was not hidden from you when I was made in the secret place, when I was woven together in the depths of the earth. Your eyes saw my unformed body all the days ordained for me were written in your book before one of them came to be (Psalm 139:13-16, NIV).

When you understand and believe how much you are loved and valued by God, you will see yourself differently. You will honor yourself and others, and see yourself in a different light. You are more than boobs and booty. More than looks. More than a sex object. God made you for a purpose—and that doesn't include being a sex symbol.

You Are Unique

God gave you innate strengths. These asset combinations are unique to each person. Some examples are achiever, communicator, focused, visionary, builder, etc. These strengths are qualities you were born with, characteristics ingrained in you. Focus on your power, developing your strengths while trusting and obeying God's Word. This practice will help you align with God's purpose. This combination positions you for an abundant life. Focus your thoughts on positive, good, admirable, and peaceful things and use your strengths to advance God's kingdom here on earth.

> So, my dear brothers and sisters, be strong and immovable. Always work enthusiastically for the Lord, for you know that nothing you do for the Lord is ever useless (1 Corinthians 15:58).

> Finally, brothers, whatever is true, whatever is honorable, whatever is just, whatever is pure, whatever is lovely, whatever is commendable, if there is any excellence, if there is anything worthy of praise, think about these things. What you have learned and received and heard and seen in me—practice these things, and the God of peace will be with you (Philippians 4:8-9, ESV).

Life is not always easy. We live in a fallen world with other imperfect people who make choices that affect everyone. Live to please God and you will have a peace in your heart that is a calming and blessed assurance.

God gives us power through the Holy Spirit to make it in this world. One of the reason's I wrote this book was to remind you of how much you are loved by God.

> Be on guard. Stand firm in the faith. Be courageous. Be strong. And do everything with love (1 Corinthians 16:13).

Many of the ladies I met while working at

the Center had similar stories of searching for love that only God can provide. It would hurt my heart to see them in such a state of confusion, sadness, and pain because of their choices. Most of my clients were deceived and misguided by the world's perceptions of femininity that bombarded them daily. I pray that the truths in this book will set free those in bondage and enslaved to sexual or other types of sin.

I pray that you believe that you are loved by God. His love is never failing, and nothing you can do will take His love away from you. Psalm 136 shows us that God's love endures forever.

> Give thanks to the Lord, for he is good. His love endures forever. Give thanks to the God of gods. His love endures forever. Give thanks to the Lord of lords: His love endures forever (Psalm 136:1-3, NIV).

> And I am convinced that nothing can ever separate us from God's love. Neither death nor life, neither angels nor demons, neither our fears for today nor our worries about tomorrow—not even the powers of hell can separate us from God's love. No power in the sky above or in the earth below—indeed, nothing in all creation will ever be able to separate us from the love of God that is revealed in Christ Jesus our Lord (Romans 8:38-39).

Think On These

- Self-worth is defined by how God loves you.
- God loves you immensely! Don't forget it.
- You are unique.
- You are fine china, strong but delicate.

Chapter 14

No More Fear Of Missing Out

Worry weighs us down; a cheerful word picks us up (Proverbs 12:25, MSG).

In the current culture, anxiety runs high. Millennials are known as the "anxious generation"[1]. This is caused by the internet and a parade of various lifestyles displayed on social media which leads women to comparisons, anxiety, and feeling overwhelmed. Decision making is hard because of the fear of missing out (FOMO).

I believe there are several reasons for these heightened emotions. The brain's prefrontal cortex, the center of judgment and reason, matures around the mid-twenties. The limbic system's emotions and feelings can overwhelm the senses and judgment because of an immature pre-frontal cortex. This may be a cause of anxiety and panic attacks experienced by some in their mid-twenties. I remember experiencing this myself in my early twenties. This new adult age is a time of change, an end to childhood and dependence. Stress is inevitable. However, it can be a good stress that drives us to move forward and start living differently.

High anxiety can also be caused by having too many available choices, especially in the dating realm. Some people fear choosing the wrong partner. The first chapter of this book, along with prayer, can help you with the decision-making process. The fear of missing out on the "right" person, house, job, city, town, vacation, or blessing can be paralyzing. This fear produces anxiety, worry, and causes people to make the choice not to choose anything at all, thus causing them to miss out on the joy of living.

I also believe there is intense, debilitating anxiety when we try to please other people to win their love or approval. Some people, maybe you are one of them, don't like confrontation or the possibility of hurting anyone. Saying no can be hard for them, even when being asked for sex. Some women think they must have sex to keep their man or to prove something to themselves or others. Here is a little secret: you cannot please everyone. Furthermore, you can't please most people. So stop trying.

When you strive to please others, anxiety follows. Trying to please people is a never-ending and futile task. This tendency is draining, toxic, and contrary to what God wants. Striving to always please others removes God from being first in your life and makes the other things an idol. You are created to put God first and be pleasing to Him. When others have a higher priority than pleasing God, it opens the door to anxiety, worry, and a host of other problems.

Anxiety Resolution

God knew anxiety, worry, and fear would be problems for us in this world and in our fallen state. When we are faced with a problem, there is always a solution in the Bible. What does the Bible say about anxiety and worry?

> Don't worry about anything; instead, pray about everything. Tell God what you need and thank him for all he has done. Then you will experience God's peace, which exceeds anything we can understand. His peace will guard your hearts and minds as you live in Christ Jesus (Philippians 4:6-7).

> Then Jesus said to his disciples: "Therefore I tell you, do not worry about your life, what you will eat; or about your body, what you will wear. For life is more than food, and the body more than clothes. Consider the ravens: They do not sow or reap, they have no storeroom or barn; yet God feeds them. And how much more valuable you are than birds! Who of you by worrying can add a single hour to your life? Since you cannot do this very little thing, why do you worry about the rest?" (Luke 12:22-26).

> Cast all your anxiety upon him, because he careth for you (1 Peter 5:7, ASV).

> For God gave us a spirit not of fear but of power and love and self-control (2 Timothy 1:7, ESV).

Have an attitude of gratitude, always giving thanks to God. It's impossible to be anxious when you are grateful. Remember the above Scriptures verses, and study to find others that you can read and hang on to. Meditate on them and pray them aloud when you feel anxious or worried. FOMO no more! Have confidence in God and yourself to make wise choices. Jesus came so you can have life to the fullest. Fear and anxiety destroy what Jesus did for you and keep you from what He yet wants you to do and be.

Be Prepared for Battle

Worry, anxiety, fear, temptation, warped cultural norms, and other things that twist God's Word are some of Satan's more effective deceptions. Remember, you are in a battle. The enemy is the prince of this world; Satan wants your soul. He relishes it when you defy God with behaviors such as people-pleasing, being anxious all the time, and having sex out of order. I hope by now you realize and accept that sex is a sacred, glorious act between a husband and wife. Satan deceives the world into believing sex is self-serving, only for pleasure, and impersonal. He is trying to take away the special covenant that sex represents and establishes. Let's not let him win!

In Ephesians 6:10-18, Paul talked about putting on the armor of God. This protection helps you to stand firm against Satan and during spiritual warfare. This armor includes:

- the shield of faith—trusting in God; protects you from doubting;
- the helmet of salvation—Jesus is your Lord and Savior;

- the breastplate of righteousness—guarding your heart; obedience to God;
- the belt of truth—truth of God's Word; all the other equipment rests on this truth;
- The shoes of the Gospel of peace—being right with God and content;
- The sword of the Spirit—an offensive weapon; the Sword is the Word of God.

The armor of God is always available, and God gives you the choice to use it. You yourself must put the armor on for it to be effective.

I put on the armor of God daily. During my morning routine, I make coffee, then read the Bible while having a cup. If there are Scriptures that resonate with me, I will write them in my journal. Then throughout the day, I pray. I use the sword of the Spirit—the Word—to protect against any toxic thoughts or negative arrows the enemy may throw my way. I keep my thoughts focused on Christ and how to be pleasing to him.

Memorizing Scripture is one of the best disciplines I have developed. It is important to know the Word. It is food for our soul, protection from the enemy, and a guide to a thriving life. I recommend keeping a favorite Scripture verse journal. Memorize as many passages as you can. Go to your journal when you need to wield your sword. Be battle ready.

Think On These

- Worry and anxiety steal from life.
- Be pleasing toward God and not people.
- Satan warps and distorts the sacredness of sex.
- Be battle ready by putting on the full armor of God.

Chapter 15

Abstinence

God's will is for you to be holy, so stay away from all sexual sin. Then each of you will control his own body and live in holiness and honor— not in lustful passion like the pagans who do not know God and his ways (1 Thessalonians 4:3-5).

"Dear Lord, what should I do? I want to be pleasing to you. Forgive me for not seeking your answers first," Lisa prayed in her heart.

"My child! Bless you for seeking Me. I want you to wait for the husband who will be in your life soon. You are My child, whom I dearly love. I want what is best for you. The powerful pleasure of sex is meant to be shared between you and your husband.

"Sex is a seal to the sacred marriage covenant. I created this action to bind you in spirit, body, and mind to your husband. You and your partner are to be intertwined with me, to help one another navigate life on earth. This is a special partnership for my Kingdom.

"I gave each of you the ability to think, choose, and feel. I can't make you choose. However, you will experience consequences for any choice you make. Some decisions can have devastating ramifications. Others can have wonderful results. Sex outside of marriage might feel good at first but will have hurtful after effects.

"When you believe in My Son, Jesus, the Holy Spirit lives in you. He helps steer you toward the right choices, if you let Him.

"I love you and I want what is best for you. Choose the path of life," God whispered to Lisa's heart.

"Thank You, Lord, for loving me. I choose life," declared Lisa.

Lisa turned to look at Kevin. He gave her a charming smile. Her heart jumped a bit. The smile didn't sway her from her decision.

"Kevin, I really like you. I enjoy spending time together."

"I really like you too," Kevin said, leaning a little closer toward her.

"I need to tell you this before things go further that I only want to have sex with my husband. I love God and want to please Him," Lisa said with godly confidence.

Kevin scooted away from her. He looked down at his hands.

Lisa couldn't read his face. She was prepared for anything that came her way.

His head raised up and he glanced over at her.

"What you just said made my feelings for you stronger. I'm experiencing a war in my head.

Should I try to have sex with you because of what's expected of me in this culture? Or do what God says and treat you as fine china, waiting until we're married?

"I too love the Lord. I respect Him and you, Lisa. Sex is worth the wait. Thank you for being honest with me.

"I had an awesome night with you. Let's defy temptation and say our goodnights. I'll get your coat and drive you home."

Lisa's heart melted. What Kevin said confirmed his good-guy status. She smiled at him and shook her head. She stood up and walked over to the door. They looked into each other's eyes, feeling the spark of everlasting love igniting in their hearts. Kevin took Lisa's hand, squeezed it, and ushered her out the door.

Although the Lisa and Kevin story is fictional, what God said to Lisa is true. He loves us and wants what is best for our lives. The Holy Spirit is our guide to an abundant life—when we give Him our life.

Self-control is a fruit of the Holy Spirit. It helps us and others to experience God's provisions. This particular fruit helps us to abstain from things that are not pleasing to God.

Just Don't Do It

There is a way to prevent us from dealing with the aftermath of sex out of order. I'm not talking about condoms or birth control, because they don't protect us from the hormonal and emotional affects. Those methods do not provide a 100% guarantee of protection against STDs. There are many stories out there of women getting pregnant while on birth control and/or using condoms. Even the little STD critters can find a way to their prey.

The only effective way to be protected from experiencing the physical, emotional, and biblical consequences of sexual sin is to not have sex! Remember, sex doesn't just mean intercourse; it is *any* intimate activity between two people that involves arousal, stimulation, and/or a response by at least one of those actions.

For sure, abstaining from sex is easier said than done. This was explained in the "Sex and the Brain" chapter. When sexual intercourse or sexual intimacy have been experienced, it is hard to stop (remember the dopamine hormone that floods our brains?). However, it can be done.

When you put all your trust in Jesus and obey His word, grace abounds and gives you the power to turn from sin. Grace gives you true freedom over sin. Jesus didn't die for you to stay in sexual sin, or any sin for that matter. You are free indeed!

Sex with your future spouse is worth the wait. You are God's creation, and He loves you so much that He gave you the guidelines to wait to have sex, so you can experience the best sex ever with your marriage partner. He also knows what heartache it can bring when you bond, attach, and break it off with other men multiple times.

Abstinence Defined

Abstinence is keeping yourself from any action or indulgence (like sex, drugs, alcohol, food), according to *The Oxford American Dictionary*. In this chapter, I define and confine it to waiting to have sex until marriage.

So How You Abstain?

If you haven't had sex, don't have sex. Wait until you have a husband. Yes, there are people who still "wait," even in today's sexually-saturated culture. It is a unique and awesome story when you hear of women (and men) waiting until they are at the altar for their first kiss! That is a true romance story. I know of a few beautiful women and handsome men who waited for their spouses.

When you save sex for marriage, you will be free from the emotional and physical pain that accompanies premarital sex. You will be proud of yourself for achieving such a significant accomplishment in the context of today's culture! Your story will be a source of encouragement to other young women and men. God will be pleased, and you will be blessed.

> For God did not call us to be impure, but to live a holy life. Therefore, anyone who rejects this instruction does not reject a human being but God, the very God who gives you his Holy Spirit (1 Thessalonians 4:7-8, NIV).

If you have had sex or are in a sexual relationship with someone, you can stop. I admit it can be difficult because of your feelings for the person and how dopamine (pleasure) and oxytocin work to promote bonding and trust. The more you have sex with the same person, the harder it will be to stop, but it can be done. If you are with someone who pressures you to have sex or disrespects you because of your decision, he is not the one you should be with. A good man will respect your decision and not try to make you change your moral decisions.

When you choose to abstain, write your declaration down, then sign and date it. Put it in a journal, on your calendar, or in a Word document and save it. Pray to God for strength, wisdom, discernment, and whatever help you need. He will guide you. Always be praying: "Commit your plans to the Lord and you will succeed" (Proverbs 16:3, NIV).

Do's and Don'ts

Do tell family members, close friends, boyfriend, pastor, or your accountability partner about your decision. If they aren't supportive, ask them to respect your decision (and get them a copy of this book).

Don't watch shows, movies, videos, or porn—things that are sexually-charged. Many of these cause arousal, especially when you are new to abstinence.

Don't read erotica or romance books that have sex scenes; these are a type of soft porn. These books, shows, and videos raise your dopamine levels. They cause the same type of arousal as sex and can even lead to addiction, making it more difficult to become aroused with your husband.

Do be aware of the type of music you listen to. Some songs may bring back memories. Others are sexually-charged and can also cause arousal!

Do be aware of who you hang out with. If they make fun of you or try to thwart your abstinence process, rethink your friendship with that person. A friend is someone who respects your decisions and helps you stay on the right path. Go back and read the healthy relationships chapters as a reminder.

Do guard your heart, mind, and eyes. Be pleasing and honoring to God in what you read and watch. When you do what is pleasing to God, your life gets better.

> The path of the righteous is like the morning sun, shining ever brighter till the full light of day. But the way of the wicked is like deep darkness; they do not know what makes them stumble (Proverbs 4:18-19, NIV).

> Above all else, guard your heart, for everything you do flows from it (Proverbs 4:23, NIV).

Do seek out a therapist, counselor, and/or medical professional if you think you are addicted to sex. This is a real and serious diagnosis; please get the help you need.

Tips and Tricks to Empower You on Your Walk in Abstinence

- Read the Bible daily.
- Trust and obey God's Word.
- Pray the Scriptures. When you read the Bible, write down verses that resonate with you Pray those Scriptures out loud over your life.
- Read.
- Write in a journal daily (Bible verses, your thoughts on the abstinence journey, etc.)
- Get an accountability partner or join a

small group of women who are walking in purity.

- Start a hobby.
- Join a gym/exercise.
- Start on that goal or dream you always wanted to do achieve.
- Hang out with friends who are supportive.
- Pray.
- Go outside and hike or pick up a sport.
- Start a blog, vlog, or podcast.
- Write a book.
- Volunteer.
- Join a small group at church. Most have a singles group and I know of a few people who have met their husbands at one.
- Talk to someone you have never talked with before (at your job, the gym, at school, etc.).
- You can still date. But remember, holding hands, back rubs, hugging, and other seemingly innocent things can flood your brain with oxytocin leading to trust and bonding.
- Pray some more.
- Find out your strengths and gifts and work on developing and expressing them. How can you use your strengths for the glory of God?

- ✿ The main thing is finding something to do that will help the lives of others. When you are helping others, you are focused on them and not on yourself or what you think you are missing.
- ✿ Did I say pray? (Prayer is very important in your walk with God!).

Don't beat yourself up if you mess up, but better yet—don't mess up. Figure out what happened to get you to that point and think of ways to protect yourself from slipping up again. Inform your accountability partner or small group. The partner or group must be honest and able, with love, to confront you with the truth if there is an issue. If the small group or partner just encourages you or is placating your failures, that will not help you grow.

God has given us the ability to choose and it's called free will. When you choose to sin, however, He doesn't save you from the consequences. Now you know the process of sex and how it is not just a pleasure trip. There are hormones working hard to get you bonded to a person, and those hormones don't care who he is. STDs are an equal opportunity problem and don't care who you are! They're just looking for a home.

You have the knowledge to make the right choice. Think of your future, your future husband, and your existing or future children. Keeping your focus on what lies ahead may help you to stay on the right track. In all you do, stay focused on Christ, seek Him and God's wisdom. Live a life yielded to Him – with righteousness through the Holy Spirit.

> Blessed are those who hunger and thirst for righteousness, for they shall be satisfied (Matthew 5:6, ESV).

I pray you choose wisely. God wants you to live an abundant life and I do too!

> Blessed is the man who walks not in the counsel of the wicked, nor stands in the way of sinners, nor sits in the seat of scoffers; but his delight is in the law of the Lord, and on his law he meditates day and night. He is like a tree planted by streams of water that yields its fruit in its season, and its leaf does not wither. In all that he does, he prospers (Psalm 1:1-3, ESV).

Five Action Steps that Must be Taken to Achieve Your Goals

Reaching a goal like abstinence, or any goal for that matter, can't be done in isolation. When you try to accomplish a mission in your own strength, you may start, but rarely reach the milestone. You need the power that only God through Jesus can provide through the Holy Spirit and with other godly supporters.

> So I say, let the Holy Spirit guide your lives. Then you won't be doing what your sinful nature craves (Galatians 5:6).

> Those who belong to Christ Jesus have nailed the passions and desires of their sinful nature to his cross and crucified them there. Since we are living by the Spirit, let us follow the Spirit's leading

in every part of our lives (Galatians 5:24-25).

An important aspect of change and reaching goals is having confidence in yourself. Believe that the change, target, or plan will be attained, even when times are tough. Determination and strong focus on the goal assists you. Have faith in God and yourself to stay on the path of life.

Your environment is a big factor in reaching your objectives. Who are you around? Do you have support? What do you watch, read, or listen to? Who are you following or liking on social media? Is your community safe? Does your community make it easy for you to reach our goals? Think of other ways your environment influences you. How would you evaluate your environment at home, work, or neighborhood?

Your motives are the last part of the equation enabling you to attain your objectives. Why do you want to make this change, goal, plan, or resolution? Is it for selfish reasons? Is it to help others? Is it to glorify God and advance His kingdom? Is it to better your health to experience the abundant life God has for you? What is your motivation?

> All the ways of a man are clean in his own sight, but the Lord weights the motive. Commit your works to the Lord and your plans will be established (Proverbs 16:2-3, NASB).

If your motivation and plans are to please and serve the Lord, they will be approved, achieved and realized. That is awesome! But it still takes work. You must make the choice. Here is the formula for success:

The Holy Spirit's leading + confidence + determination + support + let the glory of God be your motivation = Success!

If you choose abstinence, please pray the following prayer or pray your own prayer. In this prayer, there are phrases from Scripture. That's because an effective prayer is praying God's will and where better to find His will than in His Word. When you ask for something God wants, you know He hears and answers that prayer. The easiest way to pray God's will is to pray His Word with confidence.

Dear Jesus,

Thank You for all you have done, will do, and are doing in my life. I praise You because You deserve all the praise. My life is Yours. I pray to hide Your Word in my heart. You have given me a spirit of power, love, and a sound mind to accomplish great things for Your glory. Please give me the wisdom and peace that only You can give so I can choose what is best for me. Help me to do what is pleasing to You because it will be healthy for my body and refreshment for my soul. I choose to live by the Spirit. I choose life. I choose abstinence.

Strengthen my determination to accomplish this great task which my faith prompts me to make. I commit this plan to You, Lord. I know You will help me. Forgive me. I confess my sin (or sins. [Name the sin(s) you are confessing.] *I repent. Thank You for forgiving me. Don't let this sin rule in my heart, Lord. I love You. Thank You for loving me. I worship You because You are holy, good, and kind. Thank You! In Jesus' name, amen.*

Jesus can keep you from falling. Stay in communication with Him. Let me be a source for your support in the abstinence journey. I have confidence in you.

I can be reached at
Christina@SheWhoHonors.com.

Think On These

- Condoms and birth control are not 100% effective protection, nor do they protect you from the emotional consequences of sex.
- Abstinence is the best prevention.
- Abstinence is defined as keeping yourself from some action or indulgence.
- If you haven't already had sex, abstinence shouldn't be too hard.
- If you decide not to have sex until you are married, remember to write your goal down, sign it and date it!
- Read the Bible daily. Trust and obey God's Word.
- Pray. Pray. Pray!
- Follow the tips to help you on that journey and find what will help you and stick to it.
- "Commit your plans to the Lord and you will succeed" (Proverbs 16:3).
- Volunteer or regularly do something for someone else.
- Did I say pray?
- God loves you—and so do I.

Chapter 16

Lead Us Not Into Temptation

> *"And lead us not into temptation, but deliver us from evil: For thine is the kingdom, and the power, and the glory, forever. Amen"* (Matthew 6:13, KJV).

Satan is the ruler of this world, and he longs for the hearts and souls of Christ's followers to be diverted from devotion to Him. He will try his best to lure you into having sex out of order. He wants to pervert sex into a mindless animal act. Many have fallen into this tragic downward spiral, missing the powerful, mind-bending, soul-stirring, toe-curling, wonderful act between a husband and wife that God designed.

Temptations Will Arise

A few years ago, I was in a sinful situation of my own doing. An ongoing war took place in my heart. I was in a pattern of making the same wrong choice and I could not stop—or so I thought. I cried every morning in front of my children. My poor babies were so confused and sad. They didn't like to see their mom cry. Every day I prayed to the Lord, "Please, Lord, help me, I can't do this without you. I need to be removed from this temptation." I begged Him with tears flowing down my face. My heart hurt.

Then Exactly two months after the day I derailed, my phone rang. It was a call offering me a position at another job! After I hung up the phone, tears of joy streamed down my face. God had answered my prayers and removed me from the place of my temptation. I started ~~in~~ the position two weeks later.

Although removed from the temptation physically, I still had emotional and spiritual issues to fix. There were reasons I had fallen. I started seeing a Christian counselor. She helped me uncover the root cause of my choices—the "why." After exposing my hidden hurts, God started to work on me. I asked Him to forgive me. I thanked Him for forgiving me.

Not forgiving myself hindered my healing progress. Forgiving myself was key to recovery. A wall of guilt and shame for my actions was blocking God's work in my heart. Not forgiving myself also said that what Jesus did for me on the cross was not enough. I didn't want to feel that way. Forgiveness from my husband and God were lavished upon my broken heart. The power of that duo almost mended it. The one stitch missing needed to come from me.

God was on a mission. He sent Scriptures, people, books, and occurrences into my life. He pointed out His goodness, showed me His unfailing love, and showed that He accepted me—no matter what I had done.

> So now there is no condemnation for those who belong to Christ Jesus. And because you belong to him, the power of the life-giving Spirit has freed you from the power of sin that leads to death (Romans 8:1-2).

I finally forgave myself, and accepted God's forgiveness. I realized His acceptance was all I needed. As my tears streamed down my face again in a steady downpour, reminiscent of hard rainfall, I knew I was free! This was why Jesus died on the cross. I am worth dying for. The same is true for you. Jesus thought you were and are worth it.

Weapons Against Temptation

Temptations arise, but there is ammunition to combat them. God will deliver you from temptations and evil when you put on the armor of God and wield the sword of the Spirit. Believe, pray, obey, and speak His Word.

> Therefore, put on every piece of God's armor so you will be able to resist the enemy in the time of evil. Then after the battle you will still be standing firm. Stand your ground, putting on the belt of truth and the body armor of God's righteousness. For shoes, put on the peace that comes from the Good News so that you will be fully prepared. In addition to all of these, hold up the shield

of faith to stop the fiery arrows of the devil. Put on salvation as your helmet, and take the sword of the Spirit, which is the word of God (Ephesians 6:13-17).

Watch and pray that you may not enter into temptation. The spirit indeed is willing, but the flesh is weak" (Matthew 26:41, ESV).

If you think you are standing strong, be careful not to fall. The temptations in your life are no different from what others experience. And God is faithful. He will not allow the temptation to be more than you can stand. When you are tempted, he will show you a way out so that you can endure (1 Corinthians 10:12-13).

Don't let anyone under pressure to give in to evil say, "God is trying to trip me up." God is impervious to evil, and puts evil in no one's way. The temptation to give in to evil comes from us and only us. We have no one to blame but the leering, seducing flare-up of our own lust. Lust gets pregnant, and has a baby: sin! Sin grows up to adulthood, and becomes a real killer(James 1:13-15, MSG).

I never blamed God for my actions and sins. James 1:13-15 talks about giving in to temptation that comes from within us. It's true. I sinned because of what I thought was an unmet need. I harbored hurt deep in my soul. Meanwhile my need was, is, and will always be met by God's love and acceptance. Unfortunately, I had to crash to realize the truth of God's love.

> And we know that God causes everything to work together for the good of those who love God and are called according to his purpose for them (Romans 8:28).

I love what Paul wrote in Romans 8:28 and I am living proof of its truth. There are countless of miracles evidencing how God works things out for the good of those who love Him, no matter what they did.

All that I went through, good and bad choices, led me to write this book. I want you to know how much God loves you by revealing His purpose and meaning of sex and why He wants you to wait. God loves you with an everlasting love.

> And I am convinced that nothing can ever separate us from God's love. Neither death nor life, neither angels nor demons, neither our fears for today nor our worries about tomorrow—not even the powers of hell can separate us from God's love. No power in the sky above or in the earth below—indeed, nothing in all creation will ever be able to separate us from the love of God that is revealed in Christ Jesus our Lord (Romans 8:38-39).

Sex is worth waiting for.

Dear Lord,
I thank You and worship Your Holy name. Thank You for

loving me so much by giving me guidelines to help me live an abundant life, a life full of purpose. Thank You for sex and how You designed it. I pray now for Your daughters to have an open heart and mind to receive this knowledge about Your design for sex and will use it to do what is pleasing to You, oh Lord. I pray you give each woman courage and confidence to do the right thing by practicing abstinence. I pray that the knowledge of Your love for her becomes embedded in her heart, soul, and mind. I further pray she finds unspeakable joy in You and Your love, Lord. Help her to realize her worth and that she is precious in Your sight. We thank You again Lord for all that You do. You are an awesome God. In Jesus' name I pray, amen.

Chapter 17

Resources Available

I lift up my eyes to the mountains—where does my help come from?
My help comes from the Lord, the Maker of heaven and earth (Psalm 121:1-2, NIV).

My friend had a hard childhood. Her mother was emotionally absent. She never met her dad. She was the child who would fight teachers. I asked why she hit her teachers.

"I was hurting. My mom was an alcoholic and did not give me the love I needed. I never met my dad. For some reason I would take it out on my teachers. They were present and available in my life, unlike my parents," she explained.

This friend is a new Christian. We have helped each other. During a conversation, she described relationships with her other friends. I am like a sister to her, another friend is like an aunt, an older friend is a mother-figure, etc. We are her family. Although she cannot hug God, she experiences His love and help through her friends in Christ.

During that conversation, it dawned on me that yes, we are God's hands and feet. God did not leave us on earth without any help. Of course, He is the primary source of help, the Head of His Church. However, He established a spiritual family, with brothers and sisters in Christ who make up His earthly body. We are his hands and feet here on Earth.

God places what we need in our midst. We are to bring those blessings (help, money, service, listening ear, home, clothes, food, etc.) to others. There is help available for whatever you are going through: sex out of order, pregnancy, abstinence, and relationship issues, as well as Bible studies to understand the concepts of grace, forgiveness, mercy, Jesus, Christianity, and more.

The Holy Bible

As I told you earlier, I read the Bible daily. God's Word transforms, gives life, guides, corrects, and provides wisdom, peace, and comfort. Any question about life is addressed in the Bible. God's Word is truth.

I recommend the New Living Translation (NLT), New International Version (NIV), King James Version (KJV), and The Message (TMC). One-year Bibles are also an interesting way to read through it annually.

A helpful way to study the Bible is by reading one chapter at a time. For example, read the book of Romans chapter 1 on Monday, chapter 2 on Tuesday, and continue. Write down Scripture verses that speak to you. I have a journal full of Scripture that I meditate on and refer to.

PREGANCY RESOURCE CENTER MINISTRIES

There are many pregnancy resource center ministries with caring advocates to assist women in all conditions of life. Pregnant, not pregnant, mothers, single, married, men, women, young and older, Christian, non-Christian—they are a listening ear for anyone who needs it. All their services are free. These ministries are found in most cities and towns where there is a university/college.

You can email me at
Christina@shewhohonors.com
if I can help you.

National Domestic Violence Hotline:
1-800-799-7233

Website: www.thehotline.org

The Healthy Relationship First chapter provides questions and suggests steps that can lead to healthy relationships. If character red flags (angers easily, jealous of friends, etc.) are evident in the early stages, stop the relationship as soon as possible. Love is not evil and should not physically hurt.

"Domestic violence (also called intimate partner violence (IPV), domestic abuse or relationship abuse) is a pattern of behaviors used by one partner to maintain power and control over another partner in an intimate relationship." – from the National Domestic Violence Hotline website.

If you or someone you know is in a physically and/or emotionally violent relationship, please get help. You are worth it!

Beloved of God, may the truth in this book compel you to live a life of honor. Honor to Father God, honor to others and honor to yourself. You are a masterpiece created by the Most High God. He loves you. I love you, too.

About the Author

Christina Leeman is passionate about helping teen girls and young women discover their worth in God's eyes rather than from the world around them. She has a deep desire to see hearts healed and souls restored so that spirits can truly flourish. With fifteen years in ministry, she has worked with all ages—from infants to young adults—pouring into the next generation with love and wisdom.

A devoted wife to Ethan and proud mom to two daughters (and two beloved dogs), Christina finds joy in reading, exercising, and sharing laughter. Beyond ministry, she has dedicated over 24 years to healthcare, holding an MPH and certifications as a blood banker and MLT (ASCP). Whether in the lab or in the lives of those she mentors, Christina's mission remains the same: to bring hope, healing, and purpose wherever she goes.

References

Chapter 1

[1]Verhaeghe J, Gheysen R, Enzlin P. Pheromones and their effect on women's mood and sexuality. *Facts Views Vis Obgyn*. 2013;5(3):189-95.

[2]The Mind Tools Content Team. Root Cause Analysis Tracing a Problem to its Origins. https://www.mindtools.com/pages/article/newTMC_80.htm Accessed 9/1/2017

Chapter 5

[1]Barna Group. What American's believe about sex. https://www.barna.com/research/what-americans-believe-about-sex/ Accessed 1/15/2018

Chapter 7

[1]Institute for Quality and Efficiency in Health Care. How does the brain work? Pub Med Health. https://www.ncbi.nlm.nih.gov/pubmedhealth/PMH0072486/ Accessed 1/23/2018

[2]National Center for Biotechnology Information, U.S. National Library of Medicine Neurotransmitters. PubMed Health https://www.ncbi.nlm.nih.gov/pubmedhealth/PMHT0024272/ Accessed 1/23/2018

[3]Yoest KE, Cummings JA, Becker JB. Estradiol, dopamine and motivation. *Cent Nerv Syst Agents Med Chem*. 2014;14(2):83-9. https://www.ncbi.nlm.nih.gov/pmc/articles/PMC4793919/

[4]McIlhaney JS Jr, McKissic Bush F. Meet the brain In: *Hooked*. McIlhaney JS Jr, McKissic Bush F. Chicago, IL: Northfield Publishing; 2008:25-46.

[5]Field, Tiffany, et al. Breakup distress in university students. *Adolescence*. 2009;44 (176):705+. Academic OneFile, http://link.galegroup.com.clp-ezp.carnegielibrary.org/apps/doc/A217847445/AONE?u=carnegielib&sid=AONE&xid=fea6839c. Accessed 23 Jan. 2018.

[6]Kerstin Uvnäs Moberg, Francis RW. *The Oxytocin Factor : Tapping the Hormone of Calm, Love, and Healing /*. Da Capo Press, C; 2003.

[7]Peter Thorpe Ellison, Gray PB. *Endocrinology of Social Relationships*. Harvard University Press; 2009.

Chapter 8

[1]Field, Tiffany, et al. Breakup distress in university students. *Adolescence*. 2009;44 (176):705+. Academic OneFile, http://link.galegroup.com.clp-ezp.carnegielibrary.org/apps/doc/A217847445/AONE?u=carnegielib&sid=AONE&xid=fea6839c. Accessed 23 Jan. 2018.

[2]Cialdini, Robert B. Chapter 4: Social Proof: Truths are us in: *Influence the Psychology of Persuasion* Collins business essentials. Ebook.

Chapter 9

[1]Towns, Elmer L. Chapter 2 The Disciples Fast in *Fasting for Spiritual Breakthrough. A practical guide to nine Biblical fasts*. Bloomington, MN: Bethany House Publishers; 2017

[2]Brown, William E. Blessings. Bible Study Tools. https://www.biblestudytools.com/dictionaries/bakers-evangelical-dictionary/blessing.html Accessed 11/1/2018

[3]Helps Word Studies. 3107/Makarios. https://biblehub.com/str/greek/3107.htm Accessed 1/14/2019

Chapter 10

[1] Field, Tiffany, et al. Breakup distress in university students. *Adolescence.* 2009;44 (176):705+. Academic OneFile, http://link.galegroup.com.clp-ezp.carnegielibrary.org/apps/doc/A217847445/AONE?u=carnegielib&sid=AONE&xid=fea6839c.

[2] Machado Junior LC, Dalmaso ASW, Carvalho HB de. Evidence for benefits from treating cervical ectopy: literature review. *Sao Paulo Medical Journal.* 2008;126(2):132-139. doi:https://doi.org/10.1590/s1516-31802008000200014

[3] Centers for Disease Control and Prevention. Sexually Transmitted Infections Surveillance, 2022. www.cdc.gov. Published January 29, 2024. https://www.cdc.gov/std/statistics/2022/default.html

[4] CDC. About Chlamydia. Chlamydia. Published February 20, 2024. https://www.cdc.gov/chlamydia/about/index.html

[5] Centers for Disease Control and Prevention. About Gonorrhea. Gonorrhea. Published May 7, 2024. https://www.cdc.gov/gonorrhea/about/index.html

[6] CDC. About Syphilis. Syphilis. Published May 7, 2024. https://www.cdc.gov/syphilis/about/index.html

[7] American Society of Addiction Medicine. Definition of Addiction. ASAM. Published September 15, 2019. https://www.asam.org/quality-care/definition-of-addiction

[8] The Ranch TN. How Common Is Sex Addiction? The Ranch TN. Published December 24, 2016. Accessed November 10,

2024. https://www.recoveryranch.com/resources/sex-addiction-and-intimacy-disorders/sex-addiction-america-common/

[9]Zlot, Y., Goldstein, M., Cohen, K., & Weinstein, A. (2018). Online dating is associated with sex addiction and social anxiety Journal of Behavioral Addictions, 7(3), 821+. Retrieved from https://link.galegroup.com/apps/doc/A558368579/AONE?u=pl4153r&sid=AONE&xid=f9a5f8c8).

Chapter 11

[1]Arthur, Kay. *Covenant: God's Enduring Promises.* Nashville, TN: LifeWay Press; 2009

Chapter12

[1]*Strong's Concordance.* 5485. Charis. https://biblehub.com/str/greek/5485.htm Accessed 1/14/2019

[2]HELPS – Word studies. 5485.Charis. Cognate 5485, xaris. https://biblehub.com/str/greek/5485.htm Accessed 1/14/2019

Chapter 14

[1](https://www.nami.org/Blogs/NAMI-Blog/February-2019/Millennials-and-Mental-Health)